The Passion as Story

FORTRESS RESOURCES FOR PREACHING

Gerard S. Sloyan, *Worshipful Preaching*
Daniel Patte, *Preaching Paul*
Krister Stendahl, *Holy Week Preaching*
Robert G. Hughes, *A Trumpet in Darkness*
Bernard Brandon Scott, *The Word of God in Words*
John Blackwell, *The Passion as Story*

The Passion as Story
The Plot of Mark

JOHN BLACKWELL

FORTRESS PRESS   PHILADELPHIA

Library of Congress Cataloging-in-Publication Data

Blackwell, John, 1953–
  The Passion as story.

  (Fortress resources for preaching)
  1. Bible. N.T. Mark XIV–XVI—Homiletical use.
2. Jesus Christ—Passion. I. Title. II. Series.
BS2585.4.B57 1986   226´.306   85–16209
ISBN 0–8006–1144–6

1256G85   Printed in the United States of America   1–1144

to
my mentors
Burton Mack
and
Michael Winstead

Contents

Preface   9

Introduction   .   11

1. The House of the Leper—The City Slum   15

2. The Upper Room—Behind Closed Doors   25

3. The Garden—Intimations of Eden   35

4. The Temple—House of Worship   49

5. The Palace—House of Regal Splendor   61

6. The Skull—Sanctuary of Death   69

7. The Tomb—Where the Dead Do Not Live   81

Conclusion: The Passion as Story   91

Notes   95

Preface

This book is primarily for preachers. Since effective preaching cultivates faith in the imagination of the human heart, I hope that it will also be helpful to those who listen to preachers. Many regard preachers as stewards of the mysteries of Christ. These mysteries, however, are not esoteric. They are never intended to remain shrouded and concealed. The mysteries of the Bible are to be uncovered and made known.

The good sermon can be experienced as magic and often is. And yet good preaching involves no hocus-pocus! The methods by which the preacher interprets texts and prepares sermons can be learned. Preaching is never authoritative because the preacher is authoritarian. Preaching is authoritative because the sermon addresses, understands, and provides for the transformation of the human condition. The effective preacher is the one who discovers those components and movements of text and then re-creates them in a way that is imaginative and thought-provoking. Not only does the listener understand the good sermon, the listener feels understood by the good sermon.

Although there will be many occasions when I shall refer to "the preacher," I have in mind any student of the Bible. It is hoped that movements identified for sermon preparation will be useful in Bible studies as well.

I now want to thank those who have helped me during the time of preparation and writing. To Burton Mack, my New Testament teacher, I owe my ability to see the transformation in the Passion story. During my days at Claremont, he never tired of applauding and encouraging my curiosity and studies. Upon recognizing my fascination with the Passion story, he encouraged me to pursue its meaning by employing one particular method while he himself pursued Mark with other methods of interpretation. He is a remarkable teacher.

Similarly, my teaching pastor, Michael Winstead, faithfully helped me to cultivate my own communication methods, even though they were at variance with his. His tutelage is also reflected on every page of this book.

I also thank others, all of whom will be relieved to know that they are in no way held responsible for words I alone have written. Invaluable conversations with Gene and Betty Stowers motivated my reflections concerning how the Passion story shapes the life of the church. James Standiford, Hal Cowart, and Robert Lind have read the manuscript in an effort to insure its readability. Without my secretary, Pat Stulce, I should never have found the time to write. John A. Hollar, of Fortress Press, has been indefatigable in his willingness to serve as both critic and editor. He has been particularly patient in helping me to revise my style. Barry Blose, the book's copy editor, has also made helpful suggestions. Sherry Sneberger has been both humorous and tireless in typing and proofreading the manuscript. The congregation I serve as pastor has given me nothing but encouragement. Most important, my greatest supporters and cheerleaders are my wife, Nancy, and our children, Jaime and David. They stand with me always. I can never thank them enough.

Mission Bell United Methodist Church   JOHN BLACKWELL
Phoenix, Arizona
Spring 1985

Introduction

The subject of this book is the Passion story found in Mark 14:1—
16:8. What is the value of a book that addresses Mark's Passion
story? Why not interpret all of Mark? For one thing, Mark's Passion
story is a coherent story. It is the place where the entire Gospel of
Mark comes together. By understanding the Passion story, the
reader of Mark is prepared to understand the totality of the Gospel
as well. We will, however, attempt to show how earlier passages of
Mark prepare the reader for chapters 14—16. In this way, we shall
try to interpret the Passion story as the climax of the Gospel.

There are other, deeper reasons for a study that focuses on the
Passion story of Mark. This Passion story in particular features the
cross. The cross continues to serve as the symbol of the Christian
faith. Since it is difficult to imagine any component of the Christian
faith that is not embraced by the cross, the story of the cross as con-
tained in this Passion story provides a significant way to understand
the Christian faith at large. When the Christian understands the
cross with clarity, the fundamental movements of the life of faith
become clear as well.

The movements of the Christian faith are what we shall seek to
uncover in our interpretation of Mark's Passion story. We shall
attempt to explore and elucidate the movements by giving particular attention to the ways in which the characters in the story—
particularly Jesus—respond to conflict. Every effort will be made
to take the text of the story seriously on its own terms. Certain questions will constantly face the interpreter: Why does the story go this
way? How does the story help us to understand the dynamics of

conflict? How does the story help us in the resolution of conflict? And what is the significance of its outcome?

The Revised Standard Version has been used in the preparation of the book. It is hoped that before reading the interpretive material in this study the reader will become familiar with the story as Mark tells it.

Every effort will be made to exercise methodological honesty in our interpretive work. Although I have, in my own preparation, used the method of Claude Lévi-Strauss, this book is not an exercise in structuralist methodology. But it does reflect the results of my own structuralist studies in Mark, since those studies have influenced my own method.

One technical term, "symbol" (or "symbolize"), merits commentary here. A symbol discloses meaning and provokes imagination. It first facilitates one's perception of meaning: the symbol enables one to see, understand, and embrace the meaning of some large and significant reality. In what follows, we shall see that the bread and cup, as symbols, facilitate the participant's perception and understanding of Jesus' arrest and crucifixion. The bread and the cup tell the story; they portray Jesus' response to the conflicts to which he is vulnerable. In this sense, the symbol is dense: it serves as the repository of the meaning that the story conveys. As the repository of meaning, the symbol mediates meaning to the human imagination. The mediation of meaning, however, is only half the symbol's function. The symbol furthermore facilitates the conceptualization of meaning. In the case of the bread and the cup, this means that the symbol enables the recipient of the cup to conceptualize an alternative, a more appropriate response to conflict when faced with circumstances similar to those with which Jesus—the victim of rejection, betrayal, slander, and violence—is faced. The symbol impregnates the imagination. It facilitates the perception of meaning as well as the conception of meaning.

This book contains seven chapters that address seven episodes of the Passion story, each of which is primarily associated with a particular place. Since the Passion is a story, these divisions are somewhat artificial. By no means do I wish to suggest that the pericopes I have suggested represent the only division, or even the best division.

They might have been divided several ways. The divisions represented here reflect an effort to demonstrate the coherence of Mark's
Passion story.

Chapters 1–7 are each divided into two sections: "Interpreting
the Text" and "Preparing to Preach and Teach." In the interpretive
section, we shall examine the basic contours and fundamental
movements of the plot of Mark's Passion story. These fundamental
movements provide the framework for the second section. In "Preparing to Preach and Teach" I suggest approaches to the composition of the sermon or study that are concrete, while also allowing
room for the preacher's or teacher's own style and creativity to come
into play. The reader will notice that in many of the homiletical
sections I have suggested several movements for the sermon. By
using the term "movements" I am attempting to honor the different
methods of preaching that are practiced in pulpits today. It is hoped
that the various movements will be of value to both the inductive
and deductive approaches of preachers.

In the homiletical section I assume that the reader is familiar
with the material in the interpretive section. I make this assumption
because the details of the story serve as invaluable means by which
the listener is invited to participate in Mark's story. In short, "Interpreting the Text" is the cornerstone for "Preparing to Preach and
Teach." The preacher will find little value in reading the homiletical section to the exclusion of the interpretive section.

It is also hoped that those other than preachers who read this
book will find "Preparing to Preach and Teach" as valuable as the
interpretive section. Although lay people, for instance, may not
preach formally on Sunday morning, many are interested in the
Bible and some are Bible teachers. The preaching and teaching section is intended to elucidate some of the fundamental movements of
the story for all students of the Bible. This is important to note
because the movements of the story that we are isolating are
intended to coincide with the fundamental movements of human
being. "Preparing to Preach and Teach" represents at least one
effort to synchronize the movements in the story with the movements of those to whom the story is told.

By way of conclusion, we will address the significance of understanding the Passion as story. Because the Passion is story, it is appropriately understood not as the historical communication of truth but rather as the imaginative communication of truth. Thus I shall close with a word concerning the story's authority.

Finally, one should note that I am concerned with the fundamental movements of Mark's Passion story. We shall discover in the text of Mark that Jesus assumes a posture of receptivity to the people who are excluded from the life of the community and also to the events to which he becomes victim. This posture of receptivity embraces even those with whom Jesus is at odds. Jesus' kingdom-of-God vision is of a kingdom of mutual receptivity. He is so serious about this vision that he receives even those who take him by violence. By receiving them, he transforms their act of taking into an act of receiving; he transforms his being taken into a gracious giving of himself. This plot transformation not only is reflected on every page of Mark's Passion story, it is the very transformation that the Passion story engenders in the heart of the one who is willing to hear the story.

1
The House of the Leper —
The City Slum
(Mark 14:1–9)

INTERPRETING THE TEXT

The Plot to Kill Jesus

Already in the first two verses of Mark's Passion story we witness the formulation of a conspiracy, generated by a conflict that will finally result in a violent death. And at the outset, a cover-up is planned, though by the time we reach the trial and crucifixion little will remain that has not been uncovered.

The chief priests and the scribes want Jesus killed. Why? What has he done? What is he going to do? What is their motive? And why secretively? Why by stealth? These are questions of motive and conflict. Although they are provoked by the Passion story, the answers do not come easily. Mark does not say, "Here are the questions, and here are the answers."

What Mark does instead is to present certain conflicts and to associate them with certain groups of people, namely, the chief priests and the scribes. But that is all we are told. No specific motive is given. And the identities of the chief priests and scribes are unknown. Consequently, no motive can be found in any personal conflict that Jesus might have with an individual priest or scribe. We are simply told that the ones who seek Jesus' arrest are two particular groups of men.

Perhaps that is our clue. Maybe the motives that generate the conflict have nothing to do with a personal disagreement between Jesus and a particular authority. Perhaps, instead, they are related to the specific offices or functions of these two groups. The question is, Why would the *chief priests* and *scribes* want Jesus dead? Do they perceive Jesus to be in conflict with their respective offices and functions?

The priest has responsibilities with regard to worship. He functions as a mediator between the people and God. Like God, he is holy; like the people, he is a human being. He alone enters the middle section of the tabernacle, which links the people, who worship from the court, to God, who is enthroned in the holy of holies (see Exodus 29, 40; also Leviticus 8). He alone possesses the authority to decide who may participate in the cult. Does Jesus pose a threat to the chief priests' authority? Do the chief priests believe that, for reasons yet to be discovered, Jesus threatens to alter, pervert, or destroy the manner by which the priest customarily links the people to God?

The responsibility of the scribe is to interpret the law of Moses (the Pentateuch) and to teach the Lord's statutes to Israel. Failure to obey the law as interpreted by the scribe can result in banishment or death. Do the scribes, for whatever reason, feel that Jesus is in violation of the sacred order as written in the very books that they have responsibility for interpreting?

Mark has already hinted at the challenge that Jesus poses to the scribes. Jesus' teaching has authority; the scribes' does not (Mark 1:22). Jesus offers forgiveness (2:5); the scribes accuse Jesus of blasphemy (2:7) and demon possession (3:22). And yet, while the scribes, along with the chief priests and the elders, seem unable to substantiate charges that warrant his silencing, Jesus' preaching draws large crowds (2:1; 3:20; 4:1; 5:24; and 6:31).

The results are a plot and a cover-up: "It was now two days before the Passover and the feast of Unleavened Bread. And the chief priests and the scribes were seeking how to arrest him by stealth, and kill him" (14:1). But why the elaborate plot? Why the cover-up? Should Jesus violate the sacred order as they interpret and enforce it, they are clearly at liberty to have him either killed or run out of town. Unless, of course, their interpretation of sacred order is not as sacred as they have been led to believe. Should Jesus' challenge to their authority turn out to be responsible, they are in trouble. Whence comes the discord?

A Meal in the House of a Leper

Mark presents Jesus' challenge to the sacred order as interpreted by the chief priests and the scribes, in describing his association with a leper and a woman. Jesus is "in the house of Simon the leper" (14:3). This is not his first association with either a leper or a woman (see 1:40; 5:24–34; and 7:24–30). In the story of the anointing (14:3–9), however, Jesus establishes a formal association with the leper and the woman. Jesus is eating with the leper. Why should their eating together establish formal association? One does not eat with just anybody. One eats with those for whom one feels affection. Eating is the most intimate act two people can be seen in together in public. When we eat together, we are saying that we belong together. For Jesus to eat in the house of Simon the leper is for Jesus to associate himself with Simon.

This should no doubt prove horrifying to a reader in first-century Palestine: the leper was regarded as taboo (Leviticus 13—14). A disease of the skin, leprosy causes spots, eruptions, swellings, and the deterioration of the nose and ears. The leper was consequently regarded as unclean. Because of this, the leper had no part in the sacred order.

Worship, on the other hand, was to be clean and holy. To maintain a pattern of worship free from perversion, the unclean person was not permitted to have contact with the tabernacle. One who participated in the cult of sacrifice was also not permitted to have contact with an unclean person. People therefore found it necessary to distinguish the leper from other people: the leper was compelled to wear torn clothes. Torn clothes are a powerful symbol. They symbolize disgrace and exclusion from the community. Torn clothes are regarded as mocking God. Indeed, when Moses anoints Aaron and his sons priests, he says, "Do not rend your clothes, lest you die, and lest wrath come upon all the congregation" (Lev. 10:6). At all times, then, the leper had to wear torn clothes and to cover his or her upper lip and cry, "Unclean, unclean" (Lev. 13:45). Such signals would enable one to avoid contact with the leper. They would also effectively ostracize the leper not only from the tabernacle, and hence any conventional form of worship, but also from the community.

By associating with a leper in such an intimate way, Jesus is placing himself in direct conflict with the chief priests and the scribes: they alone are responsible for interpreting and enforcing the law regarding the leper. And Jesus is in violation of that law.

To make matters more complicated, a woman arrives on the scene (Mark 14:3). Women in Judaism in the time of Jesus were regarded as religiously inferior.[1] A woman had no part in public life. She had, at all times, to wear her face veiled, was never permitted to speak to a man, and if she did, brought so much disgrace upon her husband that he had the right to divorce her. In addition, "a woman had no right to bear witness."[2]

Why is this significant? Because at the outset of our story, we see Jesus, in the filthiest of first-century Palestinian slums, eating with a leper. And who should arrive on the scene but a woman, with a flask of oil, which she proceeds to break and pour over his head.

Why should that present a problem? Because the woman, who by convention has no right even to bear witness, is bearing witness to and "anointing" Jesus (making him Messiah), king over Israel.

Messiah, or Christ, means "anointed one." And this is the only time in the entire Gospel when Jesus is anointed (the women will fail to anoint Jesus at the end of the story at the tomb). Oil is a lubricant. As such, it facilitates contact between two bodies with as little friction as possible. When one is anointed, one is symbolically linked to the place where one is located (the house of a leper) and the people one is with (the leper and the woman) by what one is doing (participating in the table fellowship). As the anointed, Jesus is associated with the leper, the woman, and the leper's house.

As Messiah, Jesus also comes on behalf of the kingdom of God. There are three components in any kingdom: a king, subjects, and a social order whereby the subjects carry out the will of the king. The social order for the kingdom of God was revealed to the Israelites through Moses while the people were on their way to the promised land. It represents sacred order and time because it is regarded as relevant for all time for constituting a life of holiness.

As we have seen, Simon would have no part in the holy community. He is an outcast, ostracized because he is in violation of the perceived sacred order. In addition, because of the woman's low social position, it would seem that Mark is linking her and the leper:

although the woman is not regarded as unclean according to the Pentateuch, she is treated as religiously and socially inferior not only by the cultic staff of Jesus' time but by other males as well. For these reasons, I submit that we should understand the leper and the woman as in opposition to, or in violation of, the kingdom of God as understood by the chief priests and the scribes. By anointing Jesus in the house of Simon the leper, however, the woman is announcing and bearing witness to the fact that she, Jesus, and the leper belong together. Jesus mediates between them. Henceforth, they are included in the kingdom of God.

This brings into focus one of the motives behind the chief priests' and the scribes' wish to have Jesus killed. A motive is beginning to precipitate in the objections that are raised to the anointing. Mark does not specifically cite the *chief priests and scribes'* indignation. He simply tells us that "there were some who" were talking among "themselves indignantly" (14:4a). The juxtaposition of the statement regarding the chief priests and scribes' wish to have Jesus killed (14:1–2) with the story of the anointing links their motive to the notion of indignation over the manner of Jesus' anointing.

What are the objections? Why all this indignation? Reasons have to do with waste, the price of the oil (14:4b). It is worth three hundred denarii. A denarius equals one day's wage. Assuming one day off each week for sabbath, that would amount to an entire year's salary. That is expensive oil.

Is Mark telling us that association with Jesus is invaluable? Or is he suggesting instead that one is linked to Jesus only at great cost? After all, Mark has already hinted at this fact with excruciating poignancy: "If any man would come after me, let him deny himself and take up his cross and follow me" (8:34b).

What is clear is that because of the expense, those who witness the anointing attempt to bring reproach upon the woman: "What a waste—spending a whole year's salary just to associate herself with Jesus, when what we might have done was to take the money from this oppressed woman and give it to the poor" (au. par.).

What, then, about their motive? It masquerades as concern for the poor. Just how concerned are they? After all, Jesus responds to her objectors by telling them that they will "always have the poor"

(Mark 14:7), and that they can care for the poor whenever they are willing. How willing are they?

It seems that concern for the poor is nothing more than a front. Jesus says, "She has done a beautiful thing to me" (Mark 14:6). One who dares to call such an anointing beautiful is doomed to die: "She has anointed my body beforehand for burying" (14:8). By anointing Jesus in this particular place, this woman, who by custom is allowed to bear witness to nothing, is bearing witness to the fact that she and the leper are both linked to Jesus, the Messiah. They shall all eat together at the banquet in the kingdom of God, which now includes the house of this miserable leper.

That the inclusion of the leper and the woman should become a motive for the death of a human being is unconscionable. The exclusion of the leper and the woman from the kingdom is nothing less than insidious. The so-called sacred order is not as sacred as the chief priests and scribes have been accustomed to thinking.

And yet, by convention, only the chief priests and the scribes have the right to say so. Certainly not the woman. "And definitely not this Jesus. Who gives him such authority?! And yet—well, we'd better do away with him. But let's keep it quiet. We don't want to get caught" (au. par.).

That is why the chief priests and the scribes want Jesus dead. He not only challenges their customs and authority, he alters the very sacred order that they alone are privileged to interpret. The chief priests and the scribes view the anointing as a threat. But for Mark, it represents the gospel: "And truly, I say to you, wherever the gospel is preached in the whole world, what she has done will be told in memory of her" (14:9). The manner of one's birth or circumstances beyond one's control do not exclude one from the kingdom of God. The kingdom is not fragmented. It is whole; it is unified. The gospel—the good news—is that the woman and the leper are included. For this, Jesus is willing to die.

PREPARING TO
PREACH AND TEACH

Although exegetical preparation is an indispensable prelude to the composition of the biblical sermon, the exegesis proper is a far cry from the sermon. The preacher will in addition want to inquire as to the story's potential effect upon the imagination of the listener: What is the story about? What does it do? What problems and conditions does it address? And what components does the story introduce that effect change?

This story is about a conflict that has ruptured the kingdom of God. Certain persons have been banished from participation in the life of the community. They have been harmed, and their being harmed constitutes a violation of sacred order.

Jesus responds to the conflict by receiving his anointing as Messiah from a woman while he is at table in the house of a leper. As his anointing symbolizes the reduction of the friction that has thus far effected the ostracism of the woman and the leper, it signals the dawning of their inclusion in the sacred order. The woman and the leper are no longer outsiders. They are a part of the kingdom of God.

The anointing episode counters the vision that has thus far effected their exclusion. And yet, one still wonders why the chief priests and the scribes become so indignant over the anointing of this man by these people. After all, the woman and the leper have no recognition, let alone authority. Why should the anointing even be an issue? Why give it any attention at all? Why not ignore it?

Probably because the anointing represents truth: certain people have been inappropriately ostracized. Their exclusion has been for no good reason. Nothing authoritative can any longer force them from the kingdom of God. While Jesus' messiahship includes the woman and the leper, it reproves the chief priests and the scribes. And the chief priests and the scribes are jealous, filled with envy (15:10). Because, however, the manner of Jesus' anointing is appropriate, the chief priests and the scribes must plot to have him delivered up secretively. The so-called sacred order as they practice it is not as sacred as supposed.

Discovering what the story is about is only half the preacher's task. The preacher will also need to know how this story speaks to the conditions in which we find ourselves today. We experience similar situations. Many are yet excluded from the life of meaningful community for no legitimate reason.

The composition of the sermon might therefore examine the effects of social exclusiveness and intolerance. The preacher can paint pictures of the fragmented community: the division of the globe along national borders, the division of society along racial and economic lines, the denial of employment to the poor, the oppression of women, the exclusion of the physically disabled, and the isolation of the elderly, to name but a few. The sermon that *re-creates* the experience of isolation, alienation, banishment, and social powerlessness will be the most effective.

The exploration of the consequences of social exclusion should also expose causes. What explanations are given? By what authority? Are the reasons legitimate? Or are there underlying motives having to do with power, prestige, recognition, jealousy, and envy? Of whom are those in authority envious? What do they fear?

The sermon's examination of the effects and consequences of social exclusion can likewise offer a critique of our practices by raising questions of appropriateness. Jesus' response to the violence suffered by the kingdom of God comes in the reception of his anointing by a woman while he is at table with a leper. The introduction of the anointing experience symbolizes the reduction of the friction that has, to this point, effected the exclusion of the woman and the leper. It signals the dawning of their inclusion. This is not the first time Jesus has associated with a leper or a woman: in the very first chapter of Mark, Jesus touches a leper (1:40–45). And on the way to the house of Jairus, Jesus is touched by a woman with a hemorrhage (5:24–34). Both the woman and the leper are unclean (Lev. 13:1—15:31). Jesus converses with a woman who, because she is "a Syrophoenician by birth," is regarded by insiders as a dog (Mark 7:24–30). Mark has barely begun his story when Jesus has not only received a leper but also a paralytic, and some tax collectors, and several other sinners in his own home (2:1–17).

The anointing of Jesus (making him Messiah) presents a strong challenge to the ways in which we have customarily associated with one another. The challenge comes in the form of a new vision: sitting at table with those whom we have thus far excluded.

Events in the community in which I reside have recently provided the occasion for my preaching this text. Several Christians, two of whom are members of my own denomination, have been indicted by a federal grand jury for giving sanctuary to refugees from Central America. The people to whom I preach were anxious to know what the biblical basis for the actions of those providing sanctuary was. I wanted to show that the behavior of those who received refugees was in keeping with the gospel.

Mark 14:1-9 was my text. Using other appropriate texts from the Bible, I prepared the listener to hear the story of the anointing in the following way. (1) Drawing on the first creation story in Genesis 1, I pointed out that because God is the creator of the whole cosmos, God's concern is for the entire universe. God's concern is never limited to a single nation. National borders are the effect of human greed, symbolized by the building of a Babylonian tower in an effort to seize heaven (Gen. 11:1-9). (2) Turning to the story of the burning bush (Exodus 3), I argued that the God who is concerned for the totality of the cosmos expresses that concern in the protection of human life. (3) Referring to Matthew 25:31-46, I showed how this concern for the protection of human life is given concrete form in receiving the stranger. (4) Drawing on Matthew 5:17-20, I argued that Jesus is a respecter of law. (5) The story of the anointing in Mark 14:1-9 provided the climax of the sermon. I showed that although this story does not condone civil disobedience per se, on the occasion of his anointing as Messiah, according to Mark's story, Jesus practiced what we today would call civil disobedience. Using the details of the story, I tried to show that the anointing symbolizes the inclusion in the kingdom of God of the socially ostracized. As a part of this final movement of the sermon, I explained that those who give sanctuary to refugees, having exhausted all legal recourse and faced with a conflict of interest between the laws of the state and the sacred order in the kingdom of God, see it to be their duty to participate in the kingdom of God. For them, the choice is inescapable.

Preaching the gospel and proclaiming the kingdom of God are liable to provoke objections. How do we meet the challenge? By helping the listener to understand that people are helped by the gospel. We are never at ease with the barriers that isolate us from each other. Possessiveness provokes fear. Fear leads to devices and means for driving people away. Driving people away effects alienation. All of us fear alienation. Possessiveness, suspicion, and fear are never satisfying. Consequently, when the preacher presents a vision for the constitution of fellowship, that is a welcome enterprise. There is joy in the gospel: people embrace community.

And the courage for preaching the good news comes from the story itself. Jesus challenges the system with uncommon courage. He takes courage because he finds the notion that one be excluded from community because of the manner of one's birth or circumstances beyond one's control to be demonic. The woman and the leper are not excluded; they are "in." The strength of Jesus' belief in this truth is reflected in his willingness to die for their inclusion. That is the gospel.

2
The Upper Room—
Behind Closed Doors
(Mark 14:10–25)

The Plot to Kill Jesus

The first episode (Mark 14:1–9) began with the chief priests and scribes' seeking to kill Jesus. This episode also begins with the plot to have him "delivered up" (i.e., betrayed). In the first instance, those who want Jesus dead are the authorities; in this case, the one who wants him dead is one of the Twelve: Judas (see Mark 3:19).

Why does Judas want to deliver Jesus up? Perhaps because Judas's association with Jesus places him in direct conflict with the authorities. Judas is a friend of Jesus, one with whom Jesus eats—as are the woman and the leper. By following Jesus and participating in the table fellowship he associates himself with the anointing. The anointing resolved a conflict; it symbolized the restoration of the woman and the leper to the kingdom of God. The resolution of this conflict, however, created another one: the authority of the chief priests and the scribes and the sacred order in which they participate are confronted. This conflict will be resolved only by a violent death. No one knows this better than Judas. Unlike Jesus, who dies for the inclusion of the woman and the leper, Judas, like the chief priests and the scribes, is willing to kill for their exclusion. Judas will "hand him over," betray him.

Since Jesus is guilty of nothing, the execution of the plot will be covert. Judas will seek "an *opportunity* to betray him" (14:11). Like the chief priests and the scribes, Judas is hiding his actions. His behavior is sinister. His actions bring self-indictment.

25

A Meal in the Upper Room

The supper, according to the story, takes place "on the first day of Unleavened Bread, when they sacrificed the passover lamb" (14:12). Just as the meal at the house of the leper contrasted sacred order as practiced by the chief priests and the scribes with sacred order as initiated by Jesus' messiahship, so does the story of the meal in the upper room contrast the supper with the Feast of Unleavened Bread. Here, one needs to keep Exodus 11—12 in mind, where the unleavened bread symbolizes the escape of the people from death in Egypt. Those who sacrifice the Passover lamb are led out of Egypt. They escape with their lives before the bread has risen.

Although the supper and the Feast of Unleavened Bread should be seen together, their meanings are not the same. One serves as a mirror for the other. They must finally be contrasted.

Their contrast, however, cannot be achieved until we know something about the supper itself. What does Mark tell us? Jesus selects two of his disciples to prepare for the Passover. Which two disciples? Neither is named. The two disciples are sent into the city. Which city? Jerusalem? We are not told. They are instructed to find a man "carrying a jar of water" (14:13). What is his name? We are not told. They are instructed to follow him to a house. Its location? We are not told. They are to enter the house where they will meet a householder. But we are not told his name either. The unidentified householder will show the two unidentified disciples "a large upper room furnished" (14:15). Its location, however, shall remain a mystery. It is hidden from sight—behind closed doors.

Why does Mark tell us so little? Why is so much information withheld? An air of secrecy envelops the entire operation. What is done is deliberately secretive—closed to public view.

The preparations for the meal symbolize the plot to kill Jesus: they include the preparation of the bread, which Jesus will disclose as symbolizing his body.

And how are the preparations made? Through a contact. No name. A contact.

> Go into the city, and a man carrying a jar of water will meet you; follow him, and wherever he enters, say to the householder, "The Teacher says, Where is my guest room, where I am to eat the passover

with my disciples?" And he will show you a large upper room furnished and ready; there prepare for us. (14:13b–15)

A contact. No name. A contact. A house. Location? Unknown. Code words are spoken anonymously. Everything will be in order. There the disciples will prepare the bread; there they will "hand him over" to be killed.

It is evening. Jesus and the Twelve go to the upper room. As they sit at table, Jesus exposes the plot: "Truly, I say to you, one of you will betray me, one who is eating with me" (14:18). This saying is not unlike Psalm 41:9, which says,

> Even my bosom friend in whom I trusted,
> who ate of my bread, has lifted his heel against me.

Notice that the Passion story rearticulates this verse from the Psalter as if the same thing is happening here. In the case of Mark's Passion story, the correlation of the two experiences has to do with similarities of pattern. Both describe the human condition.

The disciples are all sorrowful; each is asking, "Is it I?" (Mark 14:19). Jesus answers, "It is one of the twelve, one who is dipping bread into the dish with me" (14:20).

In exposing the plot, Jesus then refers to himself as the Son of man: "For the Son of man goes as it is written of him, but woe to that man by whom the Son of man is betrayed!" (see Mark 8:31–33; 9:30–32; 10:32–34). As Son of man, Jesus functions as apocalyptic judge (apocalyptic meaning "uncovering"). What is Jesus uncovering? The fruit of human deed and action. The effects and consequences of human behavior, all of which are reflected in the plot. This is the human condition: one human being plots secretively to have another killed. Because of this, life is fearful and inhumane. Woe to the one who takes human life, who is self-righteous and cunning. That person would be better off having never been born; because the fruits of that person's schemes are fear, fracture, and death. Life is torn. The Son of man has disclosed this. He is the victim. This is the judgment. Jesus is the sign.

Having exposed the plot, Jesus does not then follow the plot to its logical conclusion: he does not respond to the conflict at hand according to the way people ordinarily respond to conflict. He does not resort to power, fight back, defend himself and others, or become a hero. He does not call out the army, return violence for violence, or victimize the victimizer. Instead, he transforms the plot; he introduces something new and different—an alternative response. When Jesus is actually taken to be executed (14:46), Jesus receives those who take him. He gives himself up; he transforms their act of taking into an act of receiving. Consequently, they hold in their hands not only the victim of a plot but a gift. And the gift? The gift is an approach to life that can take a situation of conflict, defuse it, and transform it into a situation of peace. Understanding his vulnerability to the point of unconditional acceptance, Jesus presents himself to his captors. He receives those who take him. He transforms his being taken into a gracious gift.

But before Jesus transforms the plot, he introduces this approach to conflict-resolution in the supper: Jesus takes bread and says, "This is my body" (14:22). How does the bread symbolize his body? Just as the bread is taken in the upper room, so will Jesus be taken in the garden. But what Jesus does with the bread he will also do in response to the plot. Just as he gives the bread to his disciples, so also will he give himself to those who come and take him. Take me; I'm yours: "Take; this is my body."

We have noted that the story of the preparations for the meal (14:12–16) symbolizes the plot "to hand over" Jesus. By this I mean that the story of the preparations represents the story of betrayal. The meaning of the plot "to hand over" Jesus has been translated into the story of the preparations for the supper. The preparations, on the one hand, and the plot to kill Jesus, on the other, reflect similar patterns. As symbol, the preparations help the participant to imagine, envision, and understand the plot. Able to envision the plot, the participant is also able to discern ways in which we deliver people up by covert plot today. As symbol, then, the story of the preparations facilitates both the perception of the meaning of betrayal in the story and the conceptualization of ways in which betrayal is practiced today. In this way, the story of the preparations is something in which we participate.

I have also suggested that the plot is transformed when, instead of following it to its logical conclusion, Jesus receives his captors. Jesus' receptivity even to those who plot to deliver him up is reflected in the story of the preparations in the following way: Jesus himself gives the instructions for the preparations. The story of the preparations represents Jesus' understanding of the human condition as well as his vulnerability to the human condition. All the rubrics in both the preparations and the meal proper reflect the transformation of an act of taking into an act of receiving, of Jesus' being taken into the giving up of himself. The effect of the story is to prepare both the participant in the supper and the one who hears the story preached, for an alternative response to conflict. The options are no longer limited to either running away and hiding or returning violence for violence. A third option is specified; the participant is free to choose.

I have already said that the story of the supper can be contrasted with the Passover and the Feast of Unleavened Bread. We now need to say something about this contrast. In the story of the Passover and the Feast of Unleavened Bread, the ones making the sacrifice escape with their lives. They take and kill the lamb, and their lives are spared. In the story of the supper, however, the one making the sacrifice loses his life. Whose life, then, is spared? The community's: those who take the bread receive into their hands a vision of that new approach that defuses a situation of conflict and violence and transforms it into a situation of peace.

I have suggested that in the supper we understand Jesus as the one making the sacrifice. One might wish to argue instead that the disciples, or the chief priests and the scribes, make the sacrifice of Jesus' life. As in the Feast of Unleavened Bread, their lives are certainly spared. The lives of the chief priests, the scribes, and the disciples, however, are not threatened. And yet, Jesus' life is threatened by those who plot to deliver him up, just as the lives of the ancient Israelites were threatened by Pharaoh. Should the reader wish to persist in suggesting the chief priests, the scribes, and the disciples as the ones who make the sacrifice, it would seem more appropriate to argue not that their lives are finally spared but that their life together is spared. Why? Because the one who takes the bread receives a new vision of a more humane approach to the resolution of conflict. The approach is the practice of receptivity—to assume a posture of openness to the contingencies to which one is vulnerable. Accepting his vulnerability and practicing receptivity, Mark's Jesus is free to die. Like Mark's Jesus, when we become free to die, we are also free to live. Death no longer determines our manner of behavior. Being a Christian does not mean that we are invulnerable to death. It means that we understand our vulnerability to death to the point of unconditional acceptance.

Because we are free to die, we are free to stand by what we believe and know to be right. We are free to receive even those who would take and kill us, because as Christ is finally raised up, so also shall our receiving others finally be exalted.

For this reason, at the conclusion of the supper, Jesus proposes a toast. What more can be done on the occasion of initiating that transformation which eases the conditions that tear life apart than to raise the wine glass together? Having given his disciples the bread, Jesus took a cup, gave thanks, and gave it to his disciples, saying,

> This is my blood of the covenant, which is poured out for many. Truly, I say to you, I shall not drink again of the fruit of the vine until that day when I drink it new in the kingdom of God. (14:24–25)

As symbol, the raising of the cup is loaded with meaning. Reading Mark 14:36, we discover that the cup has something to do with the hour of Jesus' crucifixion. For Jesus to say, "I shall not drink again of the fruit of the vine until that day when I drink it new in the kingdom of God," is for him to say that since the cup symbolizes the crucifixion, he drinks the cup when he is crucified. For Jesus to drink the cup at the meal is for him to accept the death that he will die. The crucifixion is the moment when the vision of the kingdom of God is mediated: it is the moment in Mark's story when we envision *the king*, having received those who take him, crowned with thorns and enthroned upon the cross. This is the gospel: it is written that the Messiah, the King of the Jews, will transform the plot to have himself killed, by receiving those who take him, and by being crowned, though with thorns, and enthroned, though upon a cross.

To this vision, Jesus raises the cup and gives it to his disciples. He not only celebrates, he extends an invitation to participate. That is worthy of celebration, for in this vision of the kingdom of God lies the very hope of the world for salvation from violence, fracture, fear, and despair.

> If any man would come after me, let him deny himself and take up his cross and follow me. (8:34)

Jesus' vision of the kingdom of God, then, has two major features: the restoration of the social outcast to the table of our fellowship and a reception for the one who delivers us up to death. That is the gift. Judas, it would seem, does not recognize Jesus as a gift. Consequently, Judas hands over the gift, for money, to be killed.

PREPARING TO
PREACH AND TEACH

The story of the supper addresses the problem of violence. In the story of the anointing, the plot to have Jesus killed was generated by his critique and alteration of the sacred order as interpreted by the established authorities. This conflict will be resolved only by an act of violence.

The story of the supper exposes the nature of the violent conflict by uncovering the roles of the disciples in the plot to have Jesus killed. This is done both directly, in the statement regarding Judas's hand in the plot (14:10–11), and indirectly, in the story of the supper (14:12–25).

The story further provides for the easing of the conflict of violence by introducing a response to the violent conflict that defuses and transforms it. Instead of either fleeing the scene of the crime or lording it over his captors, Jesus presents himself to them: "Let the Scriptures be fulfilled." This presentation becomes the gift both to his captors, who take his body in the garden (14:46), and to his disciples, who take the bread in the upper room (14:22). The gift bears the understanding that all humans find themselves in a condition of vulnerability to conflict. In addition, it mediates an approach to the resolution of this situation: graciously receiving those who take us.

I suggested that the story of the anointing (14:3–9) helped us understand the motives of the chief priests and the scribes for wanting Jesus dead (14:1–2) because of Mark's juxtaposition of these two episodes. For similar reasons, I suggest that the story of the supper (14:12–25) provides a motive for Judas (14:10–11) as well. Jesus' response to the conflict of violence amounts to a critique of the notion that the follower of Jesus is invulnerable to suffering and death. Judas plots to hand over Jesus either because he rejects Jesus' response to violent conflict or because he cannot comprehend Jesus' response. The tragedy is that violent conflict, which aggravates the human condition, is exacerbated because the would-be follower of Jesus rejects this Christian approach to conflict-resolution.

How might the preacher compose a sermon that is shaped by this hermeneutic? The preacher might employ the question of motive as a point of departure: Why would a follower of Jesus want him dead? Why would one follow Jesus in the first place?

By focusing on these questions, the preacher will discover that Mark provides plenty of help in raising the question. Earlier in the Gospel, the sons of Zebedee approach Jesus with a request: "Teacher, we want you to do for us whatever we ask of you. . . . Grant us to sit, one at your right hand and one at your left, in your glory" (10:35b and 37). It seems not to occur to James and John that the two who will be enthroned with Jesus, will, like him, hang from a cross (15:27). The crucifixion is his baptism; this is the cup from which Jesus drinks (10:38). The motives of James and John for allying themselves with Jesus, on the other hand, are thoroughly self-serving: they are interested in self-aggrandizement and the power to acquire.

Predictably, the ten other disciples are indignant over the presumption of James and John (10:41). By the time Jesus is confronted by his captors in the garden, however, there will hardly be a rush for seats by the throne (14:50). In the meantime, in response to James's and John's maneuvering for power and prestige, Jesus lays out his vision of discipleship in clear prose:

> You know that those who are supposed to rule over the Gentiles lord it over them, and their great men exercise authority over them. But it shall not be so among you; but whoever would be great among you must be your servant, and whoever would be first among you must be slave of all. (10:42–44)

In addition to confronting any self-aggrandizing or acquisitive motives for following Jesus, this statement also opposes the notion that being a Christian makes us invulnerable to suffering and death. Indeed, by the time James and John make their audacious request, Jesus has spelled out the Christian's vulnerability to suffering three times (8:31; 9:31; 10:33–34). And he does this "plainly" (8:32a), in public, to his disciples, and to the Twelve.

Using these passages from Mark 8—10, the preacher can uncover several motives for loyalty to Jesus: power, prestige, invulnerability to suffering and death, and the ability to acquire effortlessly. Aided by the story of the supper, the preacher can then expose the fruits of such thinking: suffering, fear, and death. The sermon thus performs the same function as Mark's Son of man: it exposes the self-aggrandizing approach to life by demonstrating its final effect, violence.

As Son of man, however, Jesus not only exposes the actions responsible for the human condition, he provides an approach for their transformation. This approach, however, is what the disciples either cannot understand or find distasteful. That is why Judas wants Jesus killed. Jesus offers his followers no protection. On the contrary, the approach Jesus advances achieves the resolution of conflict only at great expense to the disciple.

Central to the interpretive enterprise is the translation of the meaning of the biblical text into the imagination of the listener by means of the sermon. In our interpretation, we have isolated a fundamental movement, which I have wished to call the transformation in the story. That movement is Jesus' receiving his takers, presenting himself to them vulnerable. I have called this Jesus' transforming their act of taking into an act of receiving. Before they actually take him (14:46), Jesus gives himself up (14:42).

Jesus' transformation of his being taken into a giving up of himself has serious implications for the way we as Christians conduct ourselves in the face of conflict. The specter of nuclear holocaust poses the single greatest threat not only to human existence but to the entire ecosystem in which we live. Nuclear weapons are capable of both altering the genetic code and rendering the land on which we live totally inhospitable. Informed by the response to conflict found in the story of the supper, the Christian can advocate but one response to the threat of a nuclear attack: if fired upon, to give up both our land and our lives. To respond in any other fashion would be to exacerbate the problem in ways that, because they are entirely immeasurable in advance and uncontrollable, are unconscionable. Given the type of damage that nuclear weapons are capable of inflicting, any kind of nuclear retaliation would only contribute to the destruction of both the ecosystem and the fabric of human life. By responding to nuclear attack with nuclear weapons, the people victimized employ the methods of victimization in an effort to combat evil. This violates the Christian vision. By adopting the methods of evil in an effort to combat evil, we ensure that evil takes over. The quality of life degenerates, becoming both meaningless and inhumane. In view of the Christian vision as portrayed in the supper, and because life and land are of ultimate worth, a policy that includes the notion of nuclear retaliation is totally inappropriate. By contributing to the destruction of the fabric of life, a body of people expresses its contempt for the value of life.

This will leave the listener with a legitimate question: What prevents the Christian enterprise from degenerating into an exercise in masochism? The Passion story creates the ability to perceive and understand the human condition truthfully. Understanding the human condition truthfully, we are more fully able to respond to situations of conflict thoughtfully. We are better prepared to predict how our response to a situation will affect the outcome. Our actions become more deliberate and less impulsive. The possibilities for peace are increased significantly. Life becomes more humane.

3
The Garden—
Intimations of Eden
(Mark 14:26–52)

INTERPRETING THE TEXT

The Arrival at the Mount of Olives

In the previous two episodes, we have seen Mark interpreting laws and customs referring to the leper, the woman, the Passover, and the Feast of Unleavened Bread. In this episode, we again see Mark's use of the Old Testament, in Jesus' treatment of the prophet Zechariah.

Having sung a hymn, Jesus and his disciples, except Judas, go to the Mount of Olives. Upon arriving there, Jesus, in speaking to his disciples, characterizes them figuratively:

> You will all fall away; for it is written, "I will strike the shepherd, and the sheep will be scattered." But after I am raised up, I will go before you to Galilee. (Mark 14:27–28)

The disciples will "fall away," abandon Jesus (see 14:50). What are the conflicts that provoke flight? The significance of Mark's use of Zechariah, as well as his reference to the Mount of Olives, sheds some light on this question. Mark 14:27 draws from Zech. 13:7.

Zechariah 13:7 belongs to a group of oracles, which constitute the final section of Zechariah, chapters 9–14. In these chapters, the leaders of Israel are portrayed as shepherds, and the people of Israel as the shepherds' flock. The shepherds are characterized as worthless, because they have afflicted the people, fomenting disunity and undermining graciousness. Yahweh is therefore angry with the shepherds, Israel's leaders, and resolves to strike them. This results in the scattering of the sheep:

> Strike the shepherd, that the sheep may be scattered;
> I will turn my hand against the little ones.
>
> (Zech. 13:7)

Having brought down the shepherds, Yahweh can then wage battle against the nations on behalf of the sheep, the people of Israel. This battle shall be fought from "the Mount of Olives which lies before Jerusalem on the east" (Zech. 14:4); hence our reference to the Mount of Olives.

In Zechariah, the leaders of Israel are the shepherds, who, because they have been misleading the sheep, the people of Israel, are struck from outside the borders, by foreign nations that wage battle against Jerusalem. Zechariah understands this action as Yahweh's way of punishing the shepherds.

In Mark, the leaders of Israel are not portrayed as shepherds; Jesus is. As in Zechariah, Jesus is struck (crucified), but not from outside (not by the nations or by God). He is struck from within: Jesus is struck by those who in Zechariah are portrayed as both shepherds and sheep. Or, to look at the story from the perspective of Mark, those who strike Jesus are playing the role of the foreign nations in Zechariah—the outsiders. Furthermore, in Mark's schema, the disciples assume the role of the sheep; they are scattered: "And they all forsook him and fled" (14:50). In Mark, however, God does battle on behalf of no one. God does not come back and defend Jesus.

In Zechariah, the Mount of Olives provides the battleground for Yahweh's fighting on behalf of Jerusalem. In Mark, it represents a battleground of a sort; it is the place where Jesus is arrested. However, the battle never takes place. Jesus does not fight. God does not fight. And the disciples run for their lives.

Why is it important to make this observation? In Zechariah, "the Mount of Olives . . . lies before Jerusalem on the east" (Zech. 14:4). On a map of Jerusalem of New Testament times, one will note not only that the Mount of Olives is located east of the temple (as is Gethsemane) but that the activities on the Mount of Olives overlook the temple, or are related to it. On the Mount of Olives olives were grown that were processed for the oil needed in the temple.[3] The

Talmud even refers to the Mount of Olives as the Mount of Oil.[4] In addition, it has been noted that "the Mount of Olives was ploughed at the time of the second Temple," thus, associating the Mount of Olives and the temple.[5]

Since the entire Passion story has something to do with Jesus' anointing, the significance of the Mount of Olives begins to become clear: all that happens on the Mount of Olives (and in Gethsemane) will have something to do with the oil. The oil symbolizes the way in which Jesus mediates between, on the one hand, the woman and the leper, and on the other, the kingdom of God. In chapter 2, we did not note that the house of Simon the leper is located in Bethany. Bethany is located east of Jerusalem, beyond the Mount of Olives. The Mount of Olives therefore lies between the two; it narratively mediates between them. Jesus is anointed in Bethany. His anointing mediates between the leper, the woman, and the kingdom of God. The oil symbolizes their inclusion. Their inclusion provokes a conflict of violence, which will come to a head on the Mount of Olives. Just as Jesus receives his anointing in Bethany, so also will he receive those who take him on the Mount of Olives. He will give himself up.

Mark is narratively introducing a new christological system. He does this most obviously in the actions of the plot, especially in Jesus' reaction to conflict. Mark also does this less obviously in the symbols he employs: the oil, the bread, and the cup. More subtle, however, are the geographical references: opposing Bethany and Jerusalem and employing the Mount of Olives as mediating between the two, that is, *linking them*. What happens in Bethany speaks to Jerusalem; the anointing embraces Jerusalem.

Mark's introduction of a new christological system is aided by yet another geographical reference, Galilee: "But after I am raised up, I will go before you to Galilee" (Mark 14:28; cf. 16:7). In Isaiah 9 it is called "Galilee of the nations" and because of this—that is, because of its association with the nations—is held in contempt. Galilee is *not* Jerusalem; it is opposed to Jerusalem. Indeed, it has been noted that this conceptual opposition between Galilee and Jerusalem is alluded to in the Mishnah: "'The Galileans know naught of things devoted to [the use of] priests' (since few priests lived there)."[6] In the context of Mark, then, we begin to see that

Galilee is perceived to be in conflict with Jerusalem much in the
same way that Jesus is perceived to be in conflict with the priest.
This is interesting if, as one scholar contends, Galilee is "the objec-
tive of every messianic movement . . . the main seat of . . . messianic
ideas."[7] What we have here in Mark is a new messianic idea. Mark's
story constitutes an entirely new christological system. With it
comes a new way for human beings to respond to conflict and
receive people in order for life to be humane.

As would-be followers of Jesus, the disciples are invited to participate in this christological system; they are called to accept the
woman and the leper in the kingdom of God and to approach
conflict-resolution as Jesus does. Earlier in the story, the disciples
seem not to have understood this (see Mark 10:35–45). In the
present episode, we come to the place where Jesus will "give himself
up" to those who arrest him. He will receive those who seize him.
There will be no battle. There will be no extraordinary display of
power. And the disciples' loyalty to Jesus will fail.

Jesus knows this. The disciples, on the other hand, do not:

> Peter said to him, "Even though they all fall away, I will not." And
> Jesus said to him, "Truly, I say to you, this very night, before the cock
> crows twice, you will deny me three times." But he said vehemently,
> "If I must die with you, I will not deny you." And they all said the
> same. (Mark 14:29–31)

Gethsemane

Jesus and his disciples come to Gethsemane, "which lay on the
western slope of the Mount of Olives."[8] Two additional facts about
Gethsemane are important for our reading of Mark's Passion story.
One is that Gethsemane, "unlike Bethany, still [resides] within the
boundaries of greater Jerusalem."[9] The other is that "Gethsemane
means oil or perfume press." In view of what we have already said
about the Mount of Olives and the oil, Mark is again signaling that
the manner by which Jesus resolves conflict in the garden is directly
related to his mediating between outsider and insider.

Having arrived at Gethsemane, Jesus instructs his disciples: "Sit
here, while I pray" (14:32b). His instructions are simple, yet terri-
bly difficult: they invoke the disciples' undivided attention to Jesus'

agony. Through events that follow, Mark compels complete imaginative participation in the consequences of the approach Jesus is
advancing. The reader, with the disciples, is invited to look on with
open eyes.

Three disciples are singled out: Peter, James, and John. By sin-
gling out the three, not only does Mark bring the story sharply into
focus, he selects representatives of all disciples—all who claim to
follow Jesus. The three are invited to witness Jesus' agony firsthand:
"And he took with him Peter and James and John, and he began to
be greatly distressed and troubled. And he said to them, 'My soul is
very sorrowful, even unto death; remain here, and watch'"
(14:33–34). Jesus is in utter anguish. By receiving his captors, he
will be subjected to inescapable, excruciating humiliation and
pain. Jesus faces not only public mockery and injustice but torture:
"crowned" with thorns and "enthroned" on a cross, he will be
treated like a common criminal.

Although Peter, James, and John are urged to witness Jesus'
agony firsthand, Mark's telling of the story also creates some distance between the three disciples and Jesus: "And going a little far-
ther, he fell on the ground. . ." (14:35a). Jesus advances without his
disciples. He then prays "that, if it [is] possible, the hour might pass
from him" (14:35b). What is the hour? It is a figurative way of referring to the moment of his betrayal (14:41). It is related to the
moment of the crucifixion: "And it was the third hour, when they
crucified him" (15:25). "And when the sixth hour had come, there
was darkness. . ." (15:33). "And at the ninth hour Jesus cried. . ."
(15:34). For the hour to pass from Jesus would be for the very
moment of betrayal and enthronement to bypass him.

Jesus prays to God as "Abba, Father" (14:36). The term "Abba" is
Aramaic, and seems to be not unlike our term "Daddy."[10] Jesus is
relating himself to God intimately. What Jesus resolves to do, or not
to do, shall be intimately bound up in the manner in which Jesus
thinks of God and leans on God.

The Abba prayer has three major components. The first is the
notion that "all things are possible to" God (14:36; cf. 10:27).
Linked to this notion is a petition for God to remove the cup from
Jesus, the second component of the prayer. What is the cup? It is a

metaphor for Jesus' death. It is symbolized in Jesus' toast to the
manner in which he will respond to the conflict at hand. It is one
thing to toast the laying down of one's life as representative of the
kingdom of God. It is quite another actually to do the same. Temptation presents itself in the lure to abandon the enterprise. "All
things are possible?" Can God do anything? No. God cannot, and
have the story come out the way it does. By presenting himself to his
takers as vulnerable, Jesus will transform their act of taking into an
act of receiving: they will receive Jesus, just as one receives a gift.
The gift is a new approach to conflict-resolution. It will be a gift to
his captors just as it was to his followers. Had God rescued Jesus, the
gift would not have been presented. A vision of the kingdom of God
would not have been initiated. And there would have been no transformation in the story.

A transformation, however, takes place in the prayer itself. The
notion that "all things are possible" encourages the desire to escape
the contingencies to which Jesus is vulnerable: "Remove this cup
from me" (14:36). But the prayer ends on a different note. It invokes
the will of God: that the human, faced with conflict and informed
by the supper, discern the most appropriate response and act
accordingly. There are several options. Fleeing is one, but nothing
would be resolved. The conflict would only be prolonged. Fighting
is another, but that would only compound the problem. It is not
possible for God to rescue Jesus and still initiate Christianity. The
temptation, however, is to be seduced into one of these approaches.
Failure to wrestle with the consequences of either approach blinds
one to the third option.

That is how it is for Peter, James, and John. The hour of open-
eyed reflection completely bypasses them (14:40). They more or less
sleep through everything—three times (14:32–42). Jesus comes and
finds them sleeping. He singles out Peter: "Simon, are you asleep?
Could you not watch one hour? Watch and pray that you may not
enter into temptation; the spirit indeed is willing, but the flesh is
weak" (14:37b–38).

Jesus again goes away and repeats the prayer. Again the disciples
close their eyes; again they fail to pray with Jesus. A transformation
will not take place in the disciples. That they are unwilling to keep

watch with Jesus is clear. That they wish a rescue, or an abortion of the movement seems unequivocal. Perhaps it is appropriate to suggest that the three are willing to pray the first part of the prayer with Jesus: "All things are possible" (14:36a). God can do anything. Likewise, that Peter, James, and John should hope for a removal of the cup is not unlikely. On the other hand, the idea that presenting oneself vulnerable to one's captors is God's will is more than the disciples can take. They are unwilling to entertain such a possibility. So they close their eyes and sleep. They are unwilling to envision the kingdom of God.[11]

Unwilling to see, the disciples are unable to respond to Jesus. He comes a second time and questions them regarding their conduct. The disciples, however, are nonplused: "They did not know what to answer him" (14:40b).

Finally, as if to signal completion, Jesus comes yet a third time. The situation has not changed. The disciples are "still sleeping and taking [their] rest" (14:41). In speaking to them the third time, Jesus refers to himself as the Son of man:

> It is enough; the hour has come; the Son of man is betrayed into the hands of sinners. (14:41)

In the previous chapter, we noted that as Son of man, Jesus exposes the fruits of human deed and action. Here in Gethsemane, we see the human condition exposed—people take and kill others secretively. This is what Jesus uncovers. And yet there is more. As apocalyptic judge, Jesus uncovers not only the actions responsible for the human condition, but also the refusal, on the part of his followers, to entertain an approach to the human condition that will bring about its resolution.

Having invited his disciples to witness his distress and prayer, Jesus now invites them to witness his arrest: "Rise, let us be going; see, my betrayer is at hand" (14:42). Here for the second time in this episode Jesus uses language that alludes to his resurrection (cf. 14:28). When examining 14:28, we noted Mark's use of "Galilee" and its association with unorthodox messianic ideas: christological formulations that violate ways in which one thinks of the Christ— in Mark's community or ours. That these unorthodox messianic ideas are also associated with the resurrection is perhaps Mark's way of suggesting that the resurrection has to do with the exaltation of Jesus' understanding of the human condition and his response to this understanding. The disciples are asked to rise that they might see Jesus' betrayal.

Peter, James, and John do not actually betray Jesus. They do not approach the chief priests for money (Mark 14:10–11); they do not hand him over. Judas does (14:45). And yet Mark reminds us that the sleeping of Peter, James, and John is clearly associated with the actions of Judas. Mark does this by restating that Judas is "one of the twelve" (14:43), an insider. This means that although the behavior of Peter, James, and John may not be construed as betrayal proper, their actions are associated with betrayal. We suggest that their actions be understood as variations on betrayal. Their behavior is less severe. They do not fully participate with Judas, but they do not stand by Jesus. When the crisis of this episode reaches its climax, Peter, James, and John will finally abandon Jesus (14:50).

When Judas arrives on the scene, he is accompanied by "a crowd with swords and clubs, from the chief priests and the scribes and the elders" (14:43). The authorities, it seems, are attempting a cover-up. The arrest party is not something of which they are a part. They have engaged someone else to do their dirty work. Mark spells out their guilt, however, by telling us that it is they who order Jesus' arrest (14:43).

Judas also attempts to cover up his guilt. He does this by betraying Jesus with a kiss. Since this crowd does not know Jesus, it is necessary for the betrayer to identify him. The identification is in the form of a sign: "The one I shall kiss is the man; seize him and lead him away under guard" (14:44). A kiss is an expression of love; it is a way of drawing another unto oneself. Judas's betrayal of Jesus masquerades under the guise of affection for Jesus. Judas not only receives Jesus, he receives Jesus with a kiss. And yet the kiss bears as much contempt for Jesus as the spit that is directed towards him in the following episodes (14:65 and 15:19). Judas's behavior is completely shrouded by pretense, making his feigned noninvolvement in the plot perhaps the most sinister act of all.

Judas's pretense can also be seen in the way he addresses Jesus.

Upon arriving with the arrest party, Judas immediately approaches Jesus and calls him Master (14:45). Judas then kisses Jesus, and it is at this moment that the crowd lays hands on Jesus and seizes him (14:46).

Perhaps we should take note of a certain mindlessness on the part of this crowd. The crowd is duped; it merely carries out the orders of the authorities. The crowd does not know Jesus; he must be identified. Not knowing Jesus, the crowd cannot possibly be familiar with his character. And if there is any questioning on the part of the crowd as to the appropriateness of its actions, it does not enter the story. The crowd instead functions as a puppet. It permits itself to be controlled by someone else. At the same time, the actions of the crowd serve as an expression of the character of the chief priests, the scribes, and the elders. The crowd carries out the will of the authorities.

Mark presents two reactions to Jesus' arrest. The first is that of a bystander: "But one of those who stood by drew his sword, and struck the slave of the high priest and cut off his ear" (14:47). This bystander's action is somewhat ambivalent. The bystander's defense of Jesus is half-hearted: the victim, although associated with the high priest, is not truly a man of authority. He is the high priest's slave. Merely to cut off the ear of a slave does not really show serious loyalty to Jesus. The bystander's actions are at best lukewarm. They do little to defend Jesus. He does not truly stand by him.

Before portraying the second reaction to Jesus' arrest, Mark presents the question that Jesus asks of his captors:

> And Jesus said to them, "Have you come out as against a robber, with swords and clubs to capture me? Day after day I was with you in the temple teaching, and you did not seize me." (14:48)

The question exposes the absurdity of his covert betrayal by pointing out that it is just that—covert. It is done at night (14:17a), under cover. Jesus is functioning as Son of man; he is showing that his captors' actions are unconscionable: those who arrest him, and especially those behind the arrest, are hiding their actions. Indeed, they must hide their actions, for they have no legitimate grounds for pressing charges. Although many wish to criticize Jesus for his teaching, he teaches the truth. Were it otherwise, the authorities would be at liberty to arrest him openly. Instead he has become the victim of a conspiracy.

Jesus then says that his betrayal and arrest are a fulfillment of the Scriptures (14:49b). How are the Scriptures fulfilled? In chapter 3, we noted the similarity between Mark 14:18 and Psalm 41:9. Mark's Passion story rearticulates the verse from the Psalter as if the same thing is happening. We saw that Mark's correlation of the two experiences reflects a similarity of pattern. Both verses reflect the human condition. We have also seen how Mark likewise appropriates Zechariah in this episode. The shepherd is struck, and the sheep are scattered. When juxtaposed, the quotations from the Psalm and from Zechariah form a clear, terse picture of the human condition. The human condition is fragmented because some people, having perceived that another has authority, "deliver up" the other. Furthermore, the decision to defend the victim is made not so much in the interest of truth as in the interest of power and prestige. The Scriptures are fulfilled in that the sheep are scattered when the shepherd is struck—even by one of his followers—precisely because he exercises no power and offers no glory (cf. Mark 10:37). Thus they abandon Jesus: "And they all forsook him, and fled" (14:50). This is the second reaction to his arrest.

The tragedy of the human condition and the absurdity of the plot are finally represented in one sentence:

> And a young man followed him, with nothing but a linen cloth about his body; and they seized him, but he left the linen cloth and ran away naked. (14:51-52)

A young man follows Jesus. Following Jesus, he too is seized. The youth wears "nothing but a linen cloth about his body" (14:51). He is truly vulnerable. When seized, he leaves behind the cloth and flees naked. The seizure and flight vividly portray the fear associated with following Jesus (e.g., 4:35-41; 6:45-52). The vincibility and fear associated with following Jesus are tragic and pathetic. The youth has done nothing; he is a threat to no one. He is both innocent and defenseless. And yet in the melee that results from the seizure of Jesus, somebody also grabs a youth, who is left to run for his life, fully exposed.

PREPARING TO
PREACH AND TEACH

Of central importance to the episode in Gethsemane is the problem of the failure of loyalty. Knowing that serious trouble is at hand, Mark begins this portion of the story with Jesus' prediction that the eleven will abandon him. In response to Jesus' prediction, each of the eleven, following the lead of Peter, promises to stand by Jesus even unto death.

Trouble ensues. An act of violence is imminent. This presents trouble for Jesus in that he is tempted not to follow through with the approach to the resolution of the conflict that he has proposed in the supper. He prays that the hour might pass from him, and that God might remove the cup. The disciples are tempted not to pray with Jesus as he agonizes over what to do. The act of violence then takes place: Jesus is arrested. He responds to his takers by accepting their confrontation: "Rise, let us be going; see, my betrayer is at hand" (Mark 14:42). Jesus, having weighed the options, responds to the conflict of violence in the appropriate way. And the others, which I presume include the disciples, run for their lives.

One way to prepare a sermon that is faithful to this hermeneutic is to follow the fundamental movements of the text. Jesus' followers make promises. Their promises include the willingness even to die with him. Trouble then takes place. They are threatened. And in the face of trouble and threats, they pray. The prayer, if it is thoughtful and responsible, commands full reflection on and evaluation of the several options available for the resolution of the conflict. The conflict then reaches its climax. Those who are mastered by their temptations fail to respond appropriately. Those who master temptations respond appropriately.[12]

The movements of the story may be summarized: (1) promises, (2) trouble, (3) temptation and prayer (or failure to pray), (4) response. Although the fourth movement (response) represents the climax of the story, the third movement (temptation and prayer) becomes the most important component of the sermon. It is here that the options are to be fully explored and a transformation in the imagination of the listener is to take place.

The third movement (temptation and prayer) has three components. The components are found in the prayer of Jesus. The first component involves the conceptualization that "all things are possible." The preacher may wish to raise the questions, What would have happened if Jesus had fought back? What would have ensued had Jesus employed violence as a defense against his captors? Had Jesus fought back, then according to his example, every time the believer was confronted with a problem, a crisis, or a conflict, then retaliation, retribution, or vengeance would have become the standard response to effect resolution.

The second component is found in Jesus' petition for God to remove the cup (or that the hour might pass). At this point the preacher may ask, What would have happened if God had rescued Jesus in the story? Would not Jesus' response have encouraged the belief that his followers are entitled to escape the contingencies to which we are vulnerable? That we too want the hour to pass is understandable. That we too pray for the removal of the cup is excusable. Of course we want to protect our lives. Of course we are afraid of pain. Given this situation, appropriate use of the story at this point invites reflection not only on this reality, but also on the consequences of falling away and running: What happens when we are overprotective? What happens when we become possessive? What happens when we expect to be rescued every time we have a problem? Is the constitution of community truly possible under these circumstances? Is it possible to live as one together? At peace with one another? Or does life instead become inevitably fragmented? Are we then driven by suspicion, fear, acquisitive desire, and possessiveness? This component in the sermon becomes the occasion for auditing the consequences of the approach Jesus rejects.

The third component of the third movement then submits that we have a third option: to accept the contingencies to which we are vulnerable, to receive those who take us. This, however, is more than most can take. We do not ordinarily wish even to entertain such an idea. It is a horrifying thought. And yet our failure to wrestle honestly with Jesus in his prayer is to succumb to temptation. It is to close our eyes to the kingdom of God. Failure to reflect honestly is a form of betrayal. On the other hand, to participate fully in the prayer is to prepare fully for the most appropriate response. This is what the sermon can hope to do: to make people mindful.

An outline of the movements of the text would appear as follows:

1. Promises
2. Trouble
3. Temptation and Prayer
   a. All things are possible
   b. Remove the cup
   c. Thy will be done
4. Response

The fourth movement is response. Situations do arise. Conflicts inevitably threaten us. And we do respond. We do take action. Our actions, however, need not be involuntary. They may be fraught with fear. But they can nevertheless be thought through ahead of time. They can be appropriate. In this way, we pray with Jesus. We stand with him. We express loyalty.

4
The Temple—
House of Worship
(Mark 14:53–72)

INTERPRETING THE TEXT

Jesus Before the Council

In the previous episode we noted that Jesus defused a conflict of violence by receiving his captors instead of retaliating. Jesus' captors have a prisoner in their hands—a suspect. A trial will now ensue.

Jesus is led to the council. Peter follows but keeps his distance. Mark tells us that Peter goes "into the courtyard of the high priest," where he sits "with the guards" and warms himself (14:54). Peter will not witness the trial firsthand (see 14:66).

The council, on the other hand, will not only witness the trial, it will manipulate it. The high priest, the chief priests, the scribes, and the elders serve as both prosecutors and judges (14:55, 64). Indeed, at the trial before the high priest we have all the conventional leaders in the theocratic community; to suggest that a government is theocratic simply means that its leaders are divinely inspired.

The prosecution is led by the chief priests. Previously they have attempted to cover up their actions. Now they take the lead. They will seek the death penalty. To secure the death penalty, the chief priests will be in need of witnesses to testify. Mark tells us explicitly that "they found none" (14:55b). This, however, does not stop the chief priests. Instead, false witnesses are produced:

> For many bore false witness against him, and their witness did not
> agree. And some stood up and bore false witness against him, saying,

49

"We heard him say, 'I will destroy this temple that is made with hands, and in three days I will build another, not made with hands.'"
(14:56-59)

It is worth noting that, according to the Pentateuch, the minimum number of witnesses required to warrant a conviction is two (Deut. 19:15; see also Num. 35:30). Clearly, the plaintiff is severely lacking in witnesses. Not only does their testimony conflict, the council knowingly produces false witnesses. The trial before the high priest so obviously constitutes a sham that Mark's story causes the reader to wonder both at the credibility of the theocratic leaders and at the idea that any human being with even an ounce of conscience could vote to convict on such flimsy evidence. The trial will bear little resemblance to justice.

Mark next focuses on the high priest. It is clear, from the terminology, that the *high* priest is in charge of the entire priesthood. The high priest, instead of calling attention to this blatantly contradictory testimony, stands up and demands that Jesus answer his accusers. He is pathetic in obvious ways. The actions of the entire council, including the high priest, are unequivocally dishonest. The most eminent leaders of the theocratic community are condoning deceit and slander. This is nothing short of disgraceful. To say the least, the so-called divine inspiration of these leaders is being sharply criticized. A theocracy should represent the honest, well-thought-out, systematic effort to establish the kingdom of God.

As in previous episodes, Jesus' response is unconventional. He remains silent. He does not plead guilty; nor does he defend himself. He makes no answer (14:61). He does not have to answer. The high priest's actions convict the high priest. Jesus' silence accents this point. Any further word, any additional response on Jesus' part, would simply cloud the issue. The falseness and deceit of this so-called trial are so obvious that nothing else need be said.

Jesus' nonresponse suggests that the facts speak for themselves. What are the facts? That plots and actions of the council are both false and contradictory. Jesus, on the other hand, has included the leper and the woman in the kingdom of God, responded to violence as a peacemaker, and now responds to false and conflicting accusations by remaining silent. It is on these responses to the resolution of crises and conflicts that Jesus bases his claim to be Messiah.

The high priest asks Jesus if he is "the Christ [i.e., the Messiah], the Son of the Blessed" (14:61). Jesus responds: "I am; and you will see the Son of man seated at the right hand of Power, and coming with the clouds of heaven" (14:62).

At first Jesus' claim to be the Messiah might appear to be self-aggrandizing. The high priest certainly interprets it this way. Were Mark associating Jesus as apocalyptic judge with the Son of man in Daniel, the interpreter might likewise misconstrue Jesus' confession as inappropriately self-aggrandizing.

The language of Mark 14:62 is certainly reminiscent of the language that appears in Daniel 7. In Daniel 7, a king has risen against both the kingdom and the saints of "the Most High." The king has devoured not only the saints, but "the whole earth" (7:23). With the coming of the Son of man, however, the kingdom and dominion are taken away from the king:

> I saw in the night visions,
> and behold, with the clouds of heaven
>   there came one like a son of man,
> and he came to the Ancient of Days
>   and was presented before him.
> And to him was given dominion
>   and glory and kingdom,
> that all peoples, nations, and languages
>   should serve him;
> his dominion is an everlasting dominion,
>   which shall not pass away,
> and his kingdom one
>   that shall not be destroyed.
>   (Dan. 7:13–14)

While it is true that Mark's Passion story is suggesting that the kingdom is being taken from the hands of the high priest, Mark, despite employing the language of Daniel, does not characterize Jesus as Daniel characterizes the Son of man. Instead, Mark's Son of man is a Suffering Servant (see Mark 8:27–38; 9:30–37; 10:32–45).

This is not to suggest that as apocalyptic judge, Jesus is not, like the Son of man in Daniel, associated with events that are cosmic in scope. Apocalypticism, as we have seen, has to do with the uncovering of truth. As in the Passion story, Mark's apocalypse is concerned with exposing violence:

> But take heed to yourselves; for they will deliver you up to councils; and you will be beaten in synagogues; and you will stand before governors and kings for my sake, to bear testimony before them. (13:9)

And as with other apocalyptic literature, Mark's apocalypse is clearly associated with the cosmos:

> But in those days, after that tribulation, the sun will be darkened, and the moon will not give its light, and the stars will be falling from heaven, and the powers in the heavens will be shaken. And then they will see the Son of man coming in clouds with great power and glory. (13:24–26)

The apocalypse in Mark 13, however, is fulfilled in the Passion story, which immediately follows. Just as Mark's apocalypse foretells the delivering up of the human being to councils (13:9), so is Jesus delivered over to the council in the Passion story (14:53). And just as Mark's apocalypse foretells the darkening of the sun (13:24), so is the sun darkened when the Son of man is crucified (15:33). In this sense, the apocalypse in Mark points to the Passion story. The Passion story becomes paradigmatic for the disclosure of truth.

For acts of violence to be accompanied in Mark by the darkening of the cosmos is for Mark to suggest that acts of violence pervert the sacred order of the cosmos. The glory of the cosmos is not uncovered in violence and killing. Jesus as Son of man does not reveal heavenly splendor. He exposes earthly violence. He is the victim. He serves by suffering. His death itself effects the exposure of human ways and deeds that are the cause of violence.

As Son of man, Jesus is enthroned indeed. He is "seated at the right hand of Power" (14:62). But his enthronement is not a heavenly enthronement; it is an earthly enthronement on a cross. And "seated at the right hand of Power," he is not the recipient of power; he is the victim of power—power executed by those who, because they are in authority, are threatened by Jesus' allegedly self-aggrandizing claim.

The council understands none of this. The high priest responds to Jesus' confession by tearing his garments. We have already seen that torn clothes symbolize guilt, disgrace, and exclusion from the community (see chapter 1). When Moses anoints Aaron, the first high priest, and his sons, he says, "Do not rend your clothes, lest you die, and lest wrath come upon all the congregation" (Lev. 10:6; see also 21:10). For the high priest to tear his garments is for him not only to indict himself but also to remove himself from the kingdom of God. In his effort to convict Jesus the high priest convicts himself. By putting an innocent man to death he brings sin upon the entire nation. Because of his misbehavior the high priest makes himself equal to the leper.

Having torn his garments, the high priest then accuses Jesus of blasphemy. Blasphemy, the cursing and slandering of the name of God, is punishable by death (Lev. 24:16). Has Jesus committed blasphemy? Has he cursed or slandered God? Not in any overt way. He has clearly associated himself with God; he has finally laid claim to being the Messiah. But, as we have seen, he has not done this in a way that is self-aggrandizing. On the contrary, it is only at the point of his suffering, willingly serving as the victim of violence, that he lays claim to being either the Messiah or the Son of man. What, then, has Jesus slandered? He has slandered the high priest's Christology (Mark 14:62). He has negated the notion that the Messiah (Christ) is entitled to extraordinary power and to be enthroned as a military dictator. He has replaced this image with the notion that the Messiah is Messiah precisely because of his vulnerability. The true Messiah not only accepts vulnerability as integral to human being, he applauds it. His acceptance of vulnerability provides the grounds by which the Messiah envisions the appropriate resolution of conflict.

This, however, is not a vision or understanding of which the council wants any part. Having accused Jesus of blasphemy, and positing no further need of witnesses, the high priest merely asks for the council's decision (14:64). Jesus is issued a verdict of guilty and sentenced to death. And if that is not enough, some members of the council then show their contempt for Jesus by spitting on him (14:65). This is the first of several occasions when Jesus will be

mocked (see also Mark 15:16-20, 29-32). Mark 14:65 seems to pre-
suppose that as Messiah, Jesus should be able to prophesy in some
extraordinary fashion. Some members of the council not only spit
upon Jesus but cover his face and beat him, as do the guards. The
contempt of the council for Jesus and its rejection of him are thor-
ough. In the face of violence, he has neither fled nor retaliated. In
the face of accusations, he has neither pled guilty nor defended
himself. His actions have been executed solely in the interest of
appropriateness. He has shown no concern for the acquisition of
power. He has given no thought to personal prestige and glory. He
has, on the other hand, made issues of inclusion in the community
and a humane, peaceful life together a major concern. These, however, are notions that the council rejects unequivocally. His behavior
is so unlike anything they deem appropriate to the Messiah that they
will finally eliminate him entirely.

Peter in the Courtyard

The subject of Mark 14:66-72 is Peter. This is not the first we have
seen of Peter, and it is well to review some of the things Mark has
been doing with him. On the way to Caesarea Philippi (Mark
8:27-33), when Jesus asks his disciples, "Who do you say that I am?"
Peter answers correctly, "You are the Christ [i.e., Messiah]"
(8:29b). But when Jesus then teaches them "plainly" "that the Son
of man must suffer many things, and be rejected by the elders and
the chief priests and the scribes, and be killed, and after three days
rise again" (8:31), Peter not only rejects Jesus' teaching but also
begins "to rebuke" Jesus. Peter's rebuke of Jesus reflects either a misunderstanding or rejection of the Christology that Jesus promotes.
Peter's rejection of Jesus' teaching implies that the Son of man is not
vulnerable to suffering, rejection, and death. The Son of man,
according to Peter's way of thinking, is entitled to invulnerability.
Peter's christological thinking represents the thinking of other disciples as well, and it is this kind of thinking that Jesus not only rejects
but regards as demonic:

> But turning and seeing his disciples, he rebuked Peter, and said, "Get
> behind me, Satan! For you are not on the side of God, but of men."
> (8:33)

This is not the last time that Peter and the others reject the teaching of Jesus. In a second incident, Jesus again teaches them regarding the suffering, death, and rising of the Son of man (9:31), "but they did not understand the saying, and they were afraid to ask him" (9:32). Then Jesus tells the Twelve what will happen (10:32–34) and they too fail to understand.

When we come to the Passion story proper, Jesus says to Peter, "Truly, I say to you, this very night, before the cock crows twice, you will deny me three times" (14:30). Peter responds "vehemently"; he says, "If I must die with you, I will not deny you" (14:31).

In light of the threefold failure to understand Jesus' teaching with regard to the Son of man, it may be that when Peter expresses his willingness to die with Jesus he is thinking in terms of standing by and fighting with Jesus as Jesus defends his kingdom. But when Jesus then wrestles with the appropriate response to the conflict at hand (14:32–42), Peter, along with James and John, falls asleep three times. They fail to be on the watch (see Mark 13).

The story of Peter's own threefold denial of Jesus now seems to be the climax to the threefold failure to understand the Son of man and the threefold sleeping during Jesus' prayer. Peter is "below in the courtyard" (14:66). Cold and warming himself, he is approached by one of the maids of the high priest. The maid looks at Peter and accuses him of having ties to Jesus: "You also were with the Nazarene, Jesus" (14:67b). Peter responds to her accusation by denying any association with Jesus. In his denial, he says: "I neither know nor understand what you mean" (14:68). Peter then withdraws from the place where the maid confronts him but not so far that he cannot overhear conversations; Peter withdraws "into the gateway" (14:68).

The confrontation between the maid of the high priest and Peter is a private encounter—just between the two of them. After Peter withdraws, however, the maid of the high priest begins publicizing Peter's association with Jesus. Seeing Peter a second time, she begins "to say to the bystanders, 'This man is one of them'" (14:69). "But again he denied it" (14:70).

Yet a third time Peter is said to be one of Jesus' followers. This time, it is not only the maid of the high priest but the bystanders as well who associate Peter with Jesus. All eyes are on Peter; he is being publicly exposed: "Certainly you are one of them; for you are a Galilean" (14:70b).

Whereas earlier in the Gospel of Mark, Peter may be excused for misunderstanding Jesus (8:29), it is now difficult to imagine that he neither knows nor understands what the maid of the high priest means. The question is neither deep nor complicated. She simply says, "You were with Jesus" (au. par.). Likewise, when Peter denies his association with Jesus a second time, bystanders respond, "You are from Galilee" (au. par.). Given the surface, narrative level of these questions, we are led to conclude that Peter is not being truly honest. Indeed, he knows and understands enough to be dishonest; this is particularly clear when one considers that Peter has expressed his willingness to die with Jesus (Mark 14:31).

In the previous episode, we have noted Mark's use of Galilee, its association with both the resurrection and unorthodox messianic ideas. By being associated with Galilee, Peter is associated with the Christology that Jesus presents. Rather, Peter's response leaves him exposed:

> But he began to invoke a curse on himself and to swear, "I do not know this man of whom you speak." (14:71)

By invoking "a curse on himself," Peter seems to be saying, "A curse be on me if Jesus and I have ever had anything to do with each other." At this point in the story, from Peter's viewpoint, association with Jesus certainly appears to be a curse. He does not really understand the approach to the resolution of conflict that is central to Jesus' Christology. And he certainly does not participate in it. For Peter, following Jesus is a curse. The cost of discipleship is too great; the level of vulnerability is unacceptably high.

And yet, for Mark, it is because of the rejection of the Christology of Jesus by his followers that the would-be Christian community is cursed. By failing to accept the Christology of Jesus the community rejects the very gift that facilitates the amelioration of the suffering, rejection, and violence that make life unbearably inhumane.

The second crowing of the cock reminds Peter of Jesus' prediction

"Before the cock crows twice, you will deny me three times" (14:72). Having completely denied Jesus, Peter breaks down and weeps. Why? Is it because Peter, reminded by the cock's crow, suddenly remembers what he has forgotten? This is certainly possible. It may be more likely, however, that Peter suffers a breakdown because he will not understand Jesus and be faithful to the Christology Jesus initiates and practices. It may be that Peter has discovered that he has made hasty promises he cannot keep. He is unwilling to follow through; he will not participate.

PREPARING TO
PREACH AND TEACH

This rich text creates several possibilities for the composition of a sermon. It is not possible, however, to employ all the exegetical material from it; it is not even helpful to do so. For a sermon to have impact, the preacher will, like Mark, find it necessary to select certain material. I will therefore suggest one approach for selecting material.

We begin with an evaluation of the characters of the high priest, Jesus, and Peter. I have observed that the behavior of the high priest and Peter is inauthentic, as opposed to that of Jesus, which is authentic. What do I mean by authentic behavior? Behavior is authentic when it reflects what we publicly profess. All human beings practice what they truly believe. Some are able, additionally, to enunciate their true belief. Jesus' behavior is authentic in that he practices the Christology he both understands and preaches.

A sermon that contrasts the life of authenticity with a life that is inauthentic or counterfeit might re-create this contrast by focusing on the characters of Jesus, the high priest, and Peter. The sermon with this focus needs to follow the movements of the text closely.

The first movement of the sermon features the high priest. This movement should not merely describe the qualities of the high priest. It can re-create the bringing of Jesus, under arrest, to the council, the efforts to secure the death sentence, the false witnesses, the conflicting testimony, and so on. By telling the story, the preacher can portray the mockery that the council makes of justice. Having done this, the preacher can, like Mark, portray the high priest's response to the examination by the chief priests. The preacher should not only note that the trial obviously constitutes a sham but also that the high priest, instead of calling attention to the blatantly contradictory testimony of false witnesses, demands that Jesus answer his accusers. The high priest's behavior is clearly inauthentic in that, as the leader of the theocratic community, he should practice at least basic honesty. It is the high priest's responsibility to show that the plots and actions of the council are false and contradictory.

In contrast to the behavior of the high priest, and in keeping with the narrative order of the text, the second movement of the sermon should feature the response of Jesus to the accusations that are leveled against him. Although his response of silence is unconventional, it is nevertheless appropriate because the actions of both Jesus and the council speak for themselves. Whereas the council has practiced deceit and violence, Jesus has restored the leper and the woman to the kingdom of God openly and responded to violence as a peacemaker. It is on these appropriate responses to conflicts, ones that have fractured the kingdom of God, that Jesus bases his claim to be the Messiah. Since Jesus' claim is laid not so much on his preaching as on his public behavior in the face of conflict and violence, Jesus' actions must be construed as authentic in the highest sense of the term.

It would be unfair to presume that either the high priest or Jesus exemplifies most of the people to whom we preach. Few will condone the kind of dishonesty and deceit practiced by the high priest. Neither will many display the integrity of the enunciated understanding and the practice of Jesus. In view of this situation, the episode of the threefold denial by Peter provides a poignant third and final movement for a sermon that addresses the nature of inauthenticity in the life of the Christian.

Should the preacher wish to enlarge on Peter, Mark 8—10 will provide a wealth of material—in reference to the human family at large, disciples in general, the Twelve, the sacred trio—to prepare the listener to hear the episode in the courtyard. The point to be emphasized in this movement of the sermon is that Peter is being publicly associated by everybody with Jesus. The problem is that

Peter has made a promise, without fully knowing or understanding the promise. Peter apparently thought that being a follower of Jesus would entitle him to military might as well as public prestige in the kingdom (see Mark 10:35-45). If the type of Christology Jesus espouses ever becomes clear to Peter, it is a Christology that he either cannot understand or, if he can, one to which he will not be faithful. The inauthenticity for Peter is that he has pledged loyalty to Jesus, only to find out that the benefits are not at all what he expected. The result is a contradiction between what Simon Peter truly believes and what Jesus calls him to practice.

The goal of such a sermon would be to integrate an understanding of our faith and the way in which we live, particularly in response to a community plagued by conflicts of violence.

5
The Palace—
House of Regal Splendor
(Mark 15:1–20)

INTERPRETING THE TEXT

The story now moves from the trial before the high priest to the trial before Pilate (Mark 15:1–20). The chief priests, the scribes, the elders, and the whole council, having found Jesus guilty of blasphemy, a capital crime, now involve Pilate. Why do Jesus' accusers bring him to Pilate? If Jesus is indeed guilty of blasphemy, the congregation is required to stone him to death (Lev. 24:16).

Are they trying to rid themselves of the burden of guilt? Jealousy and envy seem to motivate the chief priests. We have sensed this before. But in this episode, Mark spells it out: Pilate "perceived that it was out of envy that the chief priests had delivered him up" (Mark 15:10). Earlier we saw that Jesus is anointed Messiah by a woman in the house of a leper (chapter 1). The woman and the leper were bearing witness to Jesus' messiahship. And yet, by convention they had no authority to make such a claim. The woman and the leper are outcasts. Concerning matters of the kingdom, so is Pilate.

The problem of Jesus' messiahship for the chief priests runs much deeper. It is not just that the woman and the leper point to Jesus' messiahship; they also point to serious flaws in the christological thinking of the chief priests and others in the council. The issue of authority does not merely have to do with the surface question of who has the right to anoint Jesus Messiah, or Jesus' right to claim the office of Messiah. The issue of authority raises the very question of the authoritativeness of the Christology espoused by the chief priests versus that espoused by the woman, the leper, and Jesus himself. As Messiah, Jesus is not concerned with entitlement to power.

61

As Messiah, he is concerned with questions of appropriateness: what kind of behavior is most fitting and helpful for the one in charge? These are not questions in which the council is interested. Consequently, they want Jesus eliminated. But the chief priests have not wanted publicly to give their true reasons for wanting Jesus dead. And it may be that by involving Pilate in the plot they attempt to lure someone else into carrying the guilt for Jesus' death.

Nevertheless, Mark may be making an additional suggestion by implicating not only "the temple" but also "the palace" in the plot to kill Jesus. This may be Mark's way of suggesting that, like the temple, the palace is also embraced by Jesus' messiahship. Jesus' christological approach to reality is relevant to both; it addresses both; it sheds light on both. Jesus' constitution of patterns for the ordering of life together and his approach to the resolution of conflict—particularly violent conflict—are appropriate for both the temple and the palace. Although Pilate will not reject Jesus' messiahship deliberately, neither will he embrace it. He too will bear the guilt for Jesus' execution.

Pilate asks Jesus, "Are you the King of the Jews?" (15:2). Jesus' response is curious; he once again responds in a way that is unexpected: "You have said so" (15:2; cf. 14:61). Has Pilate himself, as have the woman and the leper, said that Jesus is the King of the Jews? From Jesus' statement, it would seem so. Does this perhaps suggest that Pilate also has some sort of vested interest in eliminating Jesus? This is not a question easily answered. It does not necessarily appear so. It is clear that the high priest has allied the temple with the palace for the purpose of execution. Pilate, it seems, is being duped. His perception and response are lukewarm at best. He certainly cannot be accused of either thinking through his actions or behaving with integrity. He is not a man in charge of his own decisions and behavior. Below, Mark will write: "So Pilate, wishing to satisfy the crowd . . ." (15:15). Pilate is severely lacking in character. He appears not to understand what is going on. After Pilate asks Jesus if he is the King of the Jews, the chief priests start leveling charges against Jesus. Pilate, of course, expects Jesus to answer the charges and even asks him to do so. Jesus, however, does not. He makes "no further answer" (15:5). All this is to Pilate's bewilderment. He also fails to understand. He wonders (15:5).

In Mark 14:62 Jesus admitted to being the Messiah (Christ). We saw that this was possible because of the appropriateness with which Jesus had, to that point in the story, conducted himself and responded to conflict. At that point, when asked if he was the Messiah, silence was no longer necessary. In this episode, however, Jesus needs to say nothing further concerning the matter. All has been said. The facts speak for themselves. Anything else would only be construed as defensiveness, or even redundancy. Pilate does not understand this; but this is because he has no grasp whatsoever of the response to conflict that Jesus employs. Misunderstanding ripples. Perhaps this is why Pilate goes along with the plot. He does not understand enough to oppose the plot. His response is generated by bewilderment.

It may be that what now happens in the space created by Jesus' silence does more to expose the heinous nature of the crimes perpetrated against him (cf. Mark 15:10) than any other event. In the story of the release of Barabbas, we see what happens when passion, aggravated by the failure to understand, becomes the motivating force behind one's behavior.

On the occasion of the feast, perhaps the Feast of Unleavened Bread, the people apparently could approach the procurator and request the release of a prisoner. The Passion story further presupposes that an insurrection has taken place. For "among the rebels in prison, who had committed murder in the insurrection, there was a man called Barabbas" (15:7). Notice that in the previous episode, of the trial before the high priest, Mark has communicated Jesus' innocence indirectly: his conviction is secured only at the expense of truth and justice. In this episode, Barabbas's guilt is communicated directly. We are plainly told that Barabbas is guilty of murder.

The crowd approaches Pilate and asks him "to do as he was wont to do for them" (15:8). Pilate asks if they want him to release the King of the Jews (15:9). Note that there is no question that Jesus is the King of the Jews (see 15:12). Pilate seems to know that Jesus is innocent. Mark states explicitly that he "perceived that it was out of envy that the chief priests had delivered him up" (15:10). And yet, even understanding Jesus' innocence and the chief priests' envy, Pilate does not have the integrity to expose the plot for what it is, explain Jesus' innocence, and release him. Pilate perceives that the chief priests are envious. Perhaps he fails to understand why. And if Pilate understands either the nature of Jesus' messiahship or the plot to have him killed, Mark does not tell us so. This being the case, we are led to presume that Pilate understands very little.

The crowd, on the other hand, understands even less than Pilate. It does precisely what the chief priests tell it: "But the chief priests stirred up the crowd to have him release for them Barabbas instead" (15:11). Do both Pilate and the crowd serve as puppets, with the chief priests pulling the strings? How can so many people suspend conscience and participate in the killing of an innocent man at the obvious expense of truth and justice, even the King of the Jews? How does human perception allow for the seduction of people into such an enterprise?

In Mark's story, Jesus will be executed because he is the King of the Jews: "And Pilate again said to them, 'Then what shall I do with the man whom you call the King of the Jews?'" (15:12). Consequently, in response to Pilate's question, the crowd cries out, "Crucify him" (15:13). Pilate then answers their response with another question, "Why, what evil has he done?" (15:14a). No one, however, is willing to answer this question. No one is willing to think, to attempt to understand, to evaluate the appropriateness of what they are doing. To the question "What evil has he done?" there is no answer; there is no explanation. Jesus has done no evil; he is guilty of nothing. In their passion, however, the people are unwilling to acknowledge this. They want, instead, to kill him. They hasten to demand his execution.

It is at this point in the narrative that Mark accents Pilate's lack of character. Pilate's response is to wish merely to satisfy the crowd. He is unwilling to question the people further. If he has any genuine concern for truth or justice, he does not act out of his concern. Instead, Pilate releases Barabbas and hands Jesus over to be crucified (15:15). Whereas Barabbas, the guilty, is released, Jesus, the innocent, will be put to death. Whatever else this story may mean, its total meaning must refer to the release of the guilty at the expense of the innocent. This is what invariably happens when passion, exacerbated by the unwillingness to understand, functions as the prime mover in human response and action.

But why the difficulty in understanding? How is it possible that a crowd could prefer a murderer to a peacemaker, the guilty to the innocent? We have seen that as Messiah, Jesus responds to conflict by receiving his captors, presenting himself to them vulnerable. By presenting himself vulnerable, Jesus transforms their act of taking into an act of receiving—the receiving of a gift. The gift, as we have seen, is Jesus' response to conflict. The problem for other characters in the story, including the high priest, Pilate, the chief priests, and the crowd, is that this alternative response is so unconventional, so unlike any possibility anyone has dared to entertain, that they cannot understand it; they fail to embrace it. Jesus' response is neither retaliatory, perceived as brave and heroic, nor abortive, perceived as cowardly and ignoble. Barabbas may be guilty of violence and murder, but Jesus is guilty of violating the ways in which we customarily live our lives. It is difficult for the characters in the story to understand Jesus' approach, let alone regard it as plausible. His behavior is something with which the crowd is totally unfamiliar. Although guilty of murder, Barabbas's behavior is something with which the people are at least familiar, something they can understand. And so Barabbas is released and Jesus is held in his stead, scourged, and delivered to be crucified.

Jesus is led by soldiers into the palace (15:16). "The whole battalion" gathers (15:16). Here, Mark relates the story of the coronation of the King of the Jews. Jesus is clothed "in a purple cloak" (15:17). His crown is not of gold but of thorns. Having crowned Jesus, they mock him and salute him, "Hail, King of the Jews!" bowing and doing homage, hitting him and spitting on him. Having been rejected by the temple (14:65), Jesus is now rejected by the palace (15:19). Then, as if to drive home the point that he is being crucified *because* he is the King of the Jews, Jesus is stripped of his royal clothes and clad once again in his own clothes.

PREPARING TO
PREACH AND TEACH

Those to whom we preach frequently ask questions. Furthermore, it is difficult to imagine any Christian preacher who has not on numerous occasions been asked, "Why was Jesus rejected and killed?" In Mark's Passion story, Jesus is killed because he is the King of the Jews. But why would the people kill the King of the Jews? Or, as Pilate himself asks, "What evil has he done?" (Mark 15:14). Jesus fits none of the people's expectations with regard to what a king should be and do. He does not defend his subjects, insure their safety, show a little muscle, design a defense, and present a heroic image that is strong, mighty, glamorous, and courageous (see 15:29–32). For only a confident, courageous king inspires confidence and courage in the hearts of his subjects. Jesus does anything but this. And so, a dilemma: How can the subjects be any more heroic than their king?

Consequently, the people want him crucified. Not just the council. And not just the Jews. But a majority of the people want Jesus crucified. I bother to make this point because we continually hear of persons who want to lay the blame for Jesus' death on those associated with modern-day Judaism. We continue to witness the abuse of a kind of harmonization of the four Gospels in the interest of the perpetuation of anti-Semitism. Preachers that are responsible to Mark's Passion story in general, and to this episode in particular, will want to help people see that the guilt for the killing of Jesus cannot be assigned exclusively to the Jews. In the Passion story, almost everyone is responsible. Pilate is responsible. So is the crowd. Jesus is rejected by both the temple and the palace because his messiahship embraces not only temple and palace but also all subjects that fall under the sovereignty of these institutions. The rejection of Jesus has nothing to do with being a Jew. And the use of Mark's Passion story in defense of anti-Semitism fails to understand the Christology of Jesus in precisely the way that Pilate and the crowd have failed to understand.

Rejection of Jesus means either the failure to understand what Jesus does and why, or the unwillingness, having understood Jesus, to participate in his understanding and approach. By failing to understand the kind of christological thinking Mark seeks to cultivate in the human heart, the church, in the name of Jesus, is in danger of making lepers out of Jews or any other body with whom the church may differ. Such thinking not only is unconscionable, it categorically violates the spirit of Mark. The practice of Christianity and anti-Semitism are mutually exclusive. Faced with anti-Semitism and informed by the gospel in the Passion story, the Christian has no choice but to speak against any form of anti-Semitism as doing violence to the kingdom of God precisely because anti-Semitism represents the kind of victimization against which the Gospel of Mark speaks by conscious design.[13]

When addressing the question, Why was Jesus rejected and killed? just as it is inappropriate to blame Jews for the death of Jesus, so also is it inappropriate to victimize and alienate those to whom we preach. From our interpretation, it is clear that all of us are vulnerable to and at times guilty of rejecting Jesus precisely because the Christology to which he calls the disciple to be faithful is both difficult to understand and threatening.

This raises the question of how we structure the sermon or study. One suggestion is in order. Since the question, Why was Jesus rejected and killed? is frequently asked, the preacher or teacher can address the issue by raising the question, noting that the text itself, Mark 15:1–20, provides the occasion for asking it. In raising the question, one may wish to tell the story of the trial before Pilate just as Mark tells it. Employing this technique, the preacher or teacher will give close attention to the details of the story in search of a clue. This will invite participation in both the investigative process and the story itself. The preacher or teacher can then conclude this section of the story with the question Pilate himself asks: "Why, what evil has he done?" (15:14).

Using the Passion story, one can then show that as the King of the Jews, Jesus does not concern himself with entitlement to power; he concerns himself with questions of appropriateness. This, however, does not fit the people's expectations with regard to what a king should be and do. Consequently, they reject him.

In the final movement of the sermon or study, the preacher or teacher can retell the story of the trial before Pilate. Noting that Jesus' Christology embraces not only the temple but also the palace, one, by renarrating the details of the trial, can shed new light on the question, Why was Jesus rejected and killed? The preacher or teacher can show how Pilate, a non-Jew, was unable to comprehend Jesus' approach to conflict. When accused, Pilate expects Jesus to defend himself. Jesus does not and Pilate cannot understand Jesus' behavior. He is nonplused and bewildered. And when it then comes to Pilate's custom of releasing a prisoner on the occasion of the feast, the people ask not for the release of Jesus, the innocent, but Barabbas, the guilty. Why? Because the things of which Barabbas is guilty represent the qualities the people expect in a leader. Barabbas may be a murderer, but in situations of conflict, he knows how to behave. Comparing him with Jesus, the people seem to regard Barabbas as a hero. Jesus, on the other hand, is not heroic—at least not in the conventional sense. He may be a king, but he is the kind of king the people reject utterly. Entitlement to power and the show of strength are not his concerns. What is of concern, on the other hand, is the question of appropriate behavior. Of this king, the people want no part.

6
The Skull—
Sanctuary of Death
(Mark 15:21–39)

In the previous two episodes, we have witnessed the total disregard for issues of truth and justice. The guilty person has been released at the expense of the innocent. Barabbas may be guilty of murder, but Jesus is guilty of establishing a new order of perception and a new approach to the resolution of conflict. New orders are not easily integrated into our being. We saw this problem on the occasion of Jesus' confession before the high priest. Jesus is charged with blasphemy. It turns out, however, that what Jesus blasphemes is the high priest's Christology. For although Jesus claims to be the Messiah, and although he predicts his enthronement at the right hand of power (Mark 14:62), he is not positing his enthronement at the right hand of God as the recipient of power. On the contrary, he is saying that he shall be enthroned upon the cross as the victim of power. He adopts vulnerability as his understanding of life and a posture of receptivity as his approach to life. This vulnerability and receptivity, which are integral to the Christology of Mark's Jesus, finally bring him to the cross.

The Trip to Golgotha

The trip to Golgotha features a passer-by, Simon of Cyrene.[14] He is compelled to carry Jesus' cross (15:21). Simon of Cyrene is the third Simon we encounter. The previous two are Simon the leper (14:3–9) and Simon Peter (14:26–42, 54, 66–72). A comparison of the three suggests that one symbolizes an abortive or disjunctive

association with Jesus, namely, Simon Peter; the other two symbolize a conjunctive association with Jesus, namely, Simon the leper
and Simon of Cyrene.

Seeing the three together enhances the interpreter's understanding of a structure of Christian existence. What are the contours of
this structure? Simon Peter symbolizes the dissociation of oneself
from Jesus on the grounds that one's original expectations of Jesus'
messiahship are shattered. Simon Peter has expected that by following Jesus, he will become eligible for some type of extraordinary
power and prestige. Jesus does not meet Peter's expectations. Peter is
first unable to understand the true character of the Christology
Jesus practices. He is finally unwilling to practice the Christology
he understands. Consequently, Simon Peter denies that he and Jesus
have ever had anything to do with each other. Simon Peter, then,
represents dissociation with Jesus.

Simon the leper and Simon the Cyrene, on the other hand, symbolize the other side of the structure, what it means to be associated
with Jesus. One signals that inclusion in the kingdom of God is not
and cannot be based on either the circumstances of one's birth or the
condition of one's body; one is not excluded from the kingdom
because one is a leper. Jesus, the King of the Jews—the Christ, the
King of Israel—associates with women and lepers. The other, however, suggests that because of our association with Jesus, we might
find ourselves compelled to carry his cross (cf. Mark 8:34). Not only
is the Christian included in the kingdom of God, one as a Christian
also accepts one's own death as the final option for insuring the
inclusion of another. To be a Christian is both to be included in the
kingdom and to accept the willingness to die for the inclusion of a
fellow human being. By participating in the kingdom of God in this
way, life can become tender, humane, and free from fear, precisely
because we understand and accept life's fragility.

They bring Jesus to Golgotha. The name Golgotha "means the
place of a skull" (Mark 15:22b). Golgotha is linked narratively to
both the palace and the temple in that Golgotha—sanctuary of
death—is the site for the final execution in the plot. Here, Jesus will
be "enthroned."

The Crucifixion

Having arrived at Golgotha, Jesus is offered "wine mingled with myrrh" (15:23a). Do those who offer him the wine and myrrh wish for the king not to feel pain? For by rejecting the wine and myrrh, Jesus refuses to accept any anesthesia. There is no turning back. Jesus' refusal to be drugged is a radical departure from the sleep of Peter, James, and John in the garden. Jesus will fully experience the pain that is his to suffer.

Jesus is now crucified (15:24). And as the high priest tears his garments (14:63), and as the leper, by law, is compelled to wear "torn clothes" (Lev. 13:45), so also are Jesus' clothes now divided:

> And they crucified him, and divided his garments among them, casting lots for them, to decide what each should take. (Mark 15:24)

Torn clothes, as we have seen, symbolize exclusion from the kingdom of God because the one wearing them is a disgrace. The division of Jesus' garments symbolizes the contempt that the people have for Jesus, their belief that his Christology is unacceptable to the kingdom.

We should note that Mark 15:24 draws on Ps. 22:18:

> They divide my garments among them,
> and for my raiment they cast lots.

We shall see below that Mark employs other phrases from this psalm as well. Psalm 22 is a psalm that the tradition attributes to David (see the superscription). It depicts an occasion when David was vulnerable: helpless (Ps. 22:1), despised (22:6, 24), mocked (22:7), insulted (22:8), weak (22:15), victimized (22:16), and wounded (22:16). What Mark has done is to select a text associated with David at a moment when he is vulnerable and to link King Jesus and King David at precisely this moment. Notice, on the other hand, that Mark is not associating Jesus with portions of the tradition that characterize David with power and might. Psalm 22 does not depict the warrior David, who punishes his enemies. It instead characterizes David as one who suffers. And it is with this characterization of

David that Jesus is associated.

In Mark 15:25, we come to the first of three references to the *hour* of Jesus' crucifixion; the remaining two occur at 15:33. In the garden, Jesus had prayed that "the hour might pass from him" (14:35b). "Hour" metaphorically refers to the hour of his crucifixion, as 15:25 makes clear: "And it was the third hour when they crucified him."

Mark 15:26 says that "the inscription of the charge against him read, 'the King of the Jews.'" For the people to charge him with being the King of the Jews and to crucify him because he is the King of the Jews is for them to express their total rejection for the king and their contempt for the kingdom for which he stands. This contempt is further expressed in the verses that follow (15:27–32). Although Jesus is legally guilty of nothing, he is crucified with two robbers, "one on his right and one on his left" (15:27). For them to seat two robbers at the right and left hands of the throne is for them to say that Jesus is nothing more than a robber. Perhaps Mark is suggesting that Jesus is regarded by many as usurping their right to determine the conduct appropriate to the kingdom by introducing conduct that is unacceptable. What is clear is that there is no splendor associated with Jesus' enthronement. Enthronement is something we normally associate with glory. Glory is severely lacking in the crucifixion. Jesus is indeed seated at the right hand of power. He is not, however, seated as the recipient of power. He is enthroned as the victim of power. Therefore, the people express contempt for the king.

The passers-by, the chief priests, the scribes, and finally, the two robbers express such contempt by their behavior:

> And those who passed by derided him, wagging their heads, and saying, "Aha! You who would destroy the temple and build it in three days, save yourself, and come down from the cross!" So also the chief priests mocked him to one another with the scribes, saying, "He saved others; he cannot save himself. Let the Christ, the King of Israel, come down now from the cross, that we may see and believe." Those who were crucified with him also reviled him. (15:29–32)

First come those who pass by. They want Jesus to exercise power: "Save yourself and come down from the cross" (15:29). That Jesus is powerless can be seen once again in the portion of Psalm 22 on which Mark now draws (Ps. 22:7–8):

> All who see me mock at me,
>   they make mouths at me, they wag their heads;
> "He committed his cause to the LORD; let him deliver him,
>   let him rescue him, for he delights in him!"

Jesus is here associated with David at a time when he was mocked and humiliated. The mocking includes the charge that Jesus said he "would destroy the temple and build it in three days" (Mark 15:29). This charge is as false as the charges leveled against him at the trials before the high priest and Pilate. Nowhere in Mark's Gospel does Jesus ever make such a claim. And yet if Jesus will but come down from the cross, the people will believe. This is also true for the chief priests and the scribes: "Let the Christ, the King of Israel, come down now from the cross, that we may see and believe" (15:32). The ability to exercise power and might is what they look for in their king. Because he shows none, they are filled with contempt. The chief priests and the scribes mock Jesus "to one another," ridiculing his inability to save himself from the death he is dying. Jesus is even reviled by those with whom he is crucified. They too show their contempt for Jesus.

The narrative now makes two references to time that complement Mark 15:25: "And when the sixth hour had come, there was darkness over the whole land until the ninth hour" (15:33). Taken together, the references to the third, sixth, and ninth hours signal that the crucifixion speaks to the whole cosmos; the crucifixion embraces the entire universe: the positions of the sun at 9:00 A.M., 12:00 noon, and 3:00 P.M. sweep the cosmos. The story of the crucifixion discloses the human condition for the whole world. For there to be darkness from the time the sun is at its zenith till midafternoon is to suggest that the story of the crucifixion uncovers the dark side of human being. What is the dark side of human being? That people expect power; people believe themselves to be entitled to power. And because people believe themselves to be entitled to power, they are suspicious of anyone whom they perceive to have authority over them. Their feelings of entitlement, complicated by suspicion, generate violence, fear, and death. This is the dark side of human being.

For there to be darkness from noon till midafternoon is further-more to suggest that the story of the crucifixion literally turns the world upside down. The understanding, approach, and response that Jesus advances are totally unexpected and unconventional. The story of the crucifixion is parabolic in that it opposes an old order of reality. But it is also mythic in that it constitutes a new chart by which to plot our actions. An inversion of the world is taking place—the constitution of a new way of perceiving, understanding, and ordering life that is so revolutionary that it is symbolized narra-tively by "darkness over the whole land" not at midnight but at midday—when the sun is normally brightest.

At 3:00 P.M., Jesus then cries "with a loud voice" (15:34). His cry is a prayer: "My God, my God, why hast thou forsaken me?" (15:34). This prayer is the first line of Psalm 22. Mark again associ-ates Jesus with David at a time when David was vulnerable—forsaken by God. Why does God forsake Jesus? Why does God not come and rescue Jesus, saving him from the cross? Because if God had come and rescued Jesus, the story would have solved nothing. It would instead have undermined the approach to conflict-resolution that Mark's Jesus is initiating. It would also have established a pre-cedent in the form of a pattern of expectation: every time the Chris-tian, the follower of Jesus, was faced with a problem, a conflict, or a difficulty, the Christian would learn to expect some sort of divine, extraordinary power to rescue him or her from the situation. The Christian would regard himself or herself as entitled. Being enti-tled, the Christian would consequently become smug and compla-cent. Believing in the presence of that power, Christians would become suspicious of one another. All Christians would feel com-pelled to manifest their strength and charisma. Coercion would result. Manipulation would become the manner in which people treated one another. And this would effectively disintegrate and decompose any would-be community. The reason God has forsaken Jesus, according to Mark, is that there is no superhuman, divine power available to the Christian, and we ought not to expect it. And in the absence of this imagined power, we need no longer presume that we are at liberty, God being on our side, to harm a human being with whom we may differ. Similarly, when another human being is victimized, we need not presume that, because God will magically rescue the person in need, our standing by the person is unnecessary. Our appropriate involvement is necessary; it is an involvement that is constituted by the patterns by which Jesus conducts himself in the Passion story: practicing a posture of receptivity that embraces both the social outcast and the violent person. Our understanding and acceptance of the absence of the power of God, his forsaking Jesus, makes possible our full imaginative participation in the Passion story to the end that our behavior contributes to the easing and transforming of the human condition.

The bystanders, however, do not see it this way. When Jesus prays, "Eloi, Eloi," they think he is calling for Elijah (Mark 15:35). Elijah never died. Instead, "a chariot of fire and horses of fire separated" Elijah from Elisha. "And Elijah went up by a whirlwind into heaven" (2 Kings 2:11). Believing that Jesus is calling for Elijah, the bystanders, unlike those who tried to drug Jesus with good wine (Mark 15:23), now try to revive him with sour wine: "And one ran and, filling a sponge full of vinegar, put it on a reed and gave it to him to drink" (15:36a). Mark 15:36a draws on Ps. 69:21, another psalm that the tradition associates with David:

> They gave me poison for food,
> and for my thirst they gave me vinegar to drink.

As with Psalm 22, Psalm 69 represents a time when David is particularly vulnerable. The reason they try to revive Jesus with vinegar is that they are hoping for a rescue: "Wait, let us see whether Elijah will come to take him down" (Mark 15:36b). As the passers-by will believe if he saves himself (15:29–30), so the bystanders will believe if Elijah saves him. Notice that the bystanders, unlike the passers-by who have nothing but contempt for Jesus, remain at the cross. The bystanders are hangers-on. Like Peter, during Jesus' trial before the high priest, they remain outside in the courtyard (14:70). Here, in Golgotha, they are hoping for a last minute miracle that will confirm what they had always hoped for: a magical moment that will bring Jesus down from the cross and invest him with power. But the bystanders misunderstand. He is not calling for Elijah (Eliou). He is calling to God (Eloi). After they try to revive him with vinegar, Elijah does not rescue Jesus. Instead, Jesus utters "a loud cry" (15:37). And the moment the loud cry calls the attention of both bystander and reader of the story to Jesus, Jesus expires. Jesus breathes for the last time (15:37). The enthroned King of the Jews dies—willingly. This is the power that Mark's Passion story generates in the imagination of anyone who dares to hear Jesus' cry: the power to die.

When Jesus cries and expires, "the curtain of the temple [is] torn in two, from top to bottom" (Mark 15:38). Just as torn clothes are a symbol of disgrace and exclusion from the community, so also the tearing of the temple curtain symbolizes that the crucifixion is a disgrace to the temple. The temple authorities have promoted a Christology that is demonic precisely because it has promoted the killing of a human being. This is the disgrace. The leper, who wore torn clothes, has formerly been ostracized from the kingdom of God. The high priest, by tearing his clothes, has effected his own exclusion from the kingdom of God (cf. Lev. 10:6; Mark 14:63). Now, the tearing of the temple curtain symbolizes the exclusion of the temple from the kingdom of God because of the plot to kill, which it has generated.

One person—and one person only—acknowledges Jesus to be the Son of God. He is neither a member of the council nor one of the Twelve. Instead, he is a centurion—an outsider, a Roman, a Gentile. His confession is based on his witness of the manner in which Jesus dies. Notice the clarity of his confession: "And when the centurion, who stood facing him, saw that he thus breathed his last, he said, 'Truly this man was the Son of God!'" (Mark 15:39). The manner of Jesus' death qualifies him as the Son of God.

PREPARING TO
PREACH AND TEACH

The story of the crucifixion episode in Mark poses a challenge for Bible study and for the composition of a sermon based on it. Mark's story of the crucifixion is dense: this is the episode where the entire Passion story comes together, and the Gospel of Mark itself climaxes.

How, then, do we begin the sermon? What approaches create the kind of curiosity that sustains interest? Here are three concrete ways of getting started, all of which come from our interpretation of Mark.

First, one might simply explore the nature of Mark's Christology. Christology, of course, has to do with the way we understand, characterize, and speak of Christ. The way we characterize Christ has everything to do with the way we follow Christ—the way we live our lives, relate to other persons, respond to conflict, and so on. One way to begin the sermon or study, then, is to raise questions with regard to Mark's Christology. What qualifies Jesus as the Son of God (Mark 15:39)? What is the nature of his enthronement as the Christ? What are the contours of his kingdom? How does Jesus conduct himself? What does he say? Why are his words and behavior appropriate? How do they constitute community—our life together? Or, as Mark's community might ask, Who is the Christ, anyway?

In addressing these christological questions one ought to recognize and accentuate Jesus' full understanding and acceptance of the human vulnerability to pain and death. One can do this by lingering over the rich details of the story of the crucifixion. Vulnerability to pain and death is a reality in which we all share. Jesus accepts no anesthesia because the human being cannot protect himself or herself from vulnerability to pain and still live a life that is either meaningful or humane. Jesus' willingness to die appropriately qualifies him as the Son of God. And yet it is precisely this notion that the people reject. That is why they show contempt for Jesus as he suffers.

By contrast, our mutual acceptance of the reality of our vulnerability to suffering and death creates the possibility for a peaceful coexistence. The reasons for this are simple: when we accept the death we shall inevitably die, when we face the fact that our days are numbered, our priorities become clear. We understand that life is precious. We know that living is a privilege. Because life will one day end, it is most appropriately regarded as something to be treasured.

A second approach would be to address the question, Why did God forsake Jesus? By zeroing in on this question, one gains an appreciation for and understanding of Mark's Passion plot. Why did God not rescue Jesus? Why does the story go the way it does? Help in raising these questions comes from Mark himself.

One might answer the question in several movements: the first movement raises the question, Why did God forsake Jesus? Here one re-creates the scene, drawing on Mark 15:21–27. The second movement focuses the contempt that the passers-by, the chief priests, the scribes, and the robbers show for Jesus. Should Jesus show force and strength and save himself, they are willing to believe.

The third movement addresses the references to time—the signif-icance of darkness from noon till midafternoon (15:33). We have seen that this darkness signals that the story uncovers the dark side of human being—that people feel entitled. In the Gospel of Mark, several persons feel entitled to special privilege and favor because of their position. James and John think that, because they are mem-bers of the Twelve, they are entitled to sit at the right and left hands of Jesus' throne (10:35–45). In addition, the chief priests and the scribes believe that only they can make decisions with regard to who is "in" and who is "out."

We are faced with similar situations in the world today. Apart-heid is widely regarded by Christians as demonic. And yet we Christians are also vulnerable to the belief that because we are Christian, or because we were born citizens of the country in which we live, we are entitled to its wealth, to the exclusion of those who are not born under similar circumstances. This feeling of entitle-ment often comes in the form of paying mere lip service to the notion of inclusive communities. Feelings of entitlement take the form of believing that we have earned everything we have, forget-ting that we were privileged with the position of being able to acquire our possessions. This attitude provokes the refusal to admit strangers onto the land on which we live. We too often believe that because of the circumstances of our birth, we are entitled to the privileges we enjoy.

The portrayal of the consequences of feelings of entitlement pre-pares the listener for the fourth movement, where we answer the question, Why did God forsake Jesus? The preacher or teacher will want to convey that had God rescued Jesus in the story, the rescue not only would have solved nothing, but it also would have established a dangerous precedent: the story would have led the follower of Jesus to presume that God will rescue him or her when faced with a difficult situation; the Passion story would create the illusion of our invulnerability to suffering and death.

In the fifth movement one should juxtapose the response of the bystanders to Jesus' prayer. Unlike the passers-by, the bystanders do not show contempt for Jesus. They are hangers-on; they politely wait for a rescue attempt. The passers-by, however, misunderstand totally. Thinking, instead, that Jesus is calling Elijah, they attempt to sustain him long enough for the rescue to take place.

In the sixth and final movement one would contrast the tearing of the temple curtain (15:38) with the confession of the centurion (15:39). By making this contrast, like Mark, one observes a contrast between the disgrace associated with expectations of power and the plot to kill, and the true precedent that is initiated by Mark's plot: the willingness to die for the inclusion of another human being.

This, then, is the order of the second approach to reading and preaching the Markan crucifixion episode:

1. Raise the question, Why did God forsake Jesus?
2. Re-create the contempt for Jesus
3. Explain the references to time
4. Answer the question, Why did God forsake Jesus?
5. Deal with the response of the bystanders
6. Contrast the temple and the centurion episodes

A third approach to the Markan crucifixion episodes could take into account the contrast of the three Simons—Simon Peter, Simon the leper, and Simon of Cyrene. The first Simon, Simon Peter, symbolizes dissociation from Jesus. The second two, Simon the leper and Simon of Cyrene, symbolize association with Jesus. Taken together, they constitute what I call a structure of Christian existence. Reflecting or sermonizing on this theme could follow a schema in two parts:

1. Dissociation with Jesus—Simon Peter
2. Association with Jesus
    A. Simon the leper
    B. Simon of Cyrene

By focusing on Simon Peter, one addresses the components of dissociation with Jesus. While focusing on the portrayal of Simon Peter in the Passion story, one would also turn back to the episode of Peter's confession at Caesarea Philippi (Mark 8:27–33). In so doing both Simon Peter's misunderstanding of Jesus and his unwillingness, in the end, to follow Jesus because of the vulnerability associated with the practice of Jesus' Christology are seen most clearly.

Association with Jesus has two movements. Drawing on the story of Jesus' anointing by the woman, the first movement demonstrates that association with Jesus means inclusion in the community. The second movement suggests that association with Jesus also means vulnerability to the obligation to carry the cross of Christ (cf. 8:34; 15:21). Here one relives and retells the story of the crucifixion, conveying the significance of Jesus' willingness to receive both the social outcast and those who would kill him because he so acts. His willingness to practice receptivity initiates the kingdom of God. Reflection on and preaching this receptivity give birth to the vision of the kingdom of God in the human heart.

7
The Tomb—
Where the Dead Do Not Live
(Mark 15:40—16:8)

INTERPRETING THE TEXT

The Burial of the Corpse

The first episode of Mark's Passion story featured a woman who anointed Jesus. The anointing signaled the dawn of the inclusion of the woman and other social outcasts in the kingdom of God. Unlike Peter, who dissociated himself from Jesus, and other members of the Twelve who forsook Jesus and fled, the woman who anointed Jesus associated herself completely with Jesus' messiahship. This messiahship would finally result in the violent death of the Messiah, leaving his followers defenseless.

The woman who anoints Jesus Messiah is not the only woman who follows Jesus. At the scene of his execution, "there were also women looking on from afar, among whom were Mary Magdalene, and Mary the mother of James the younger and of Joses, and Salome" (15:40). These women have been following Jesus and ministering to him throughout his entire Galilean ministry (15:41). Mark further states that there were "also many other women who came up with him to Jerusalem" (15:41).

The second woman listed in 15:40 is Mary *the mother* of James the younger and of Joses. Similarly, Mark has also told the reader that Simon the Cyrene is *the father* of Alexander and Rufas (15:21). Notice that although Mark says nothing concerning the significance of the offspring of Mary the mother and of Simon of Cyrene the father, Mark's wording narratively associates the two. Simon of Cyrene, as we have seen, carries Jesus' cross, and the three women, of which one is Mary the mother, follow Jesus not only throughout his Galilean ministry, but all the way to the cross. The involvement of the women not only is positive, it is far superior to the sleeping of Peter, James, and John. The narrative association between the women and Simon of Cyrene suggests that because the women look on *from afar*, they participate in spite of their vulnerability to being compelled to carry Jesus' cross.

These women are also the ones who attempt, unsuccessfully, to anoint the corpse of Jesus. The story of Joseph of Arimathea (15:42–47), however, intervenes between their presence at the cross (15:40–41) and at the tomb (16:1–8). Mark's careful wording, Joseph *of Arimathea*, links him to Simon *of Cyrene*. The line of reasoning would be similar to that which linked Simon of Cyrene the father, to Mary the mother. Simon of Cyrene carries the cross upon which Jesus is killed. Once Jesus is dead, Joseph of Arimathea asks for his corpse—to carry it to burial.

Mark tells us that it is evening of "the day of Preparation, that is, the day before the sabbath" (15:42). Joseph of Arimathea is "a respected member of the council" (15:43). As a "respected member of the council," one might expect Joseph to honor the Sabbath. Sabbath begins on the day of Preparation with the setting of the sun. Any work is strictly forbidden; the Sabbath is a day of rest (see Gen. 2:1–3; Exod. 16:22–36; 20:8–11; 23:12). And yet, Joseph of Arimathea approaches Pilate and asks for Jesus' corpse. Since it is evening, Joseph's actions should constitute not only a violation of the Sabbath but also a violation of the spirit of the actions of the council—of which he is a member. Why might Joseph of Arimathea willingly place himself in such a vulnerable position? He is "looking for the kingdom of God." The council has failed to participate in the kingdom of God; the council has failed to integrate community; the council has failed to mobilize truth and justice. Perhaps the reason Joseph takes courage in both violating the Sabbath and approaching Pilate is that the institution of the Sabbath has failed as well. It has not cultivated the kind of reflection necessary for perceiving and living in the kingdom of God. Mark's Passion story does not appear to consider sabbatical violation inappropriate (cf. Mark 2:23–28; 3:1–6). It appears, rather, that Mark's story regards the institution of the Sabbath a failure precisely because it has not effectively generated a clear understanding of the human condition. Therefore, Joseph of Arimathea is willing to take the risk of breaking with status-quo religious practice.

Mark 15:43 represents the first time in the Passion story that Mark speaks of courage. We have sensed before that all the actions of Jesus are courageous; it would be difficult to imagine anyone's accusing him of being a coward. We have also sensed that the behavior of the women is courageous—particularly when contrasted with the flight of the disciples. In telling of Joseph's approach to Pilate "for the body of Jesus," Mark explicitly says that Joseph takes "courage" (15:43). His behavior poses a serious challenge to his colleagues. He is taking a very unpopular position.

Pilate, surprised to learn that Jesus has already died (15:44; cf. 15:5), summons the centurion who has witnessed Jesus' expiration to inquire about Jesus' death. Upon learning that Jesus has indeed died, Pilate grants the body to Joseph. Joseph purchases a shroud, takes Jesus down from the cross, wraps his body, and lays "him in a tomb which had been hewn out of rock" (15:46). A stone is rolled "against the door of the tomb" for security (15:46). Finally, Mary Magdalene and Mary the mother see "where he was laid" (15:47), thus preparing us for the final episode.

Notice that the way in which Mark composes the story invites the interpreter to contrast the role of Joseph of Arimathea with the actions of Judas. Just as Judas, a member of the Twelve, is singled out, so also is Joseph, "a respected member of the council." Joseph's role is almost the exact opposite of Judas's. Judas hands over the live body of Jesus to be violently killed. Once Jesus is dead, Joseph asks for the corpse of Jesus for burial. Why does Joseph ask for the corpse of Jesus? Because he is looking for the kingdom of God.

What does asking for the corpse of Jesus have to do with looking for the kingdom of God? The corpse of Jesus epitomizes the human condition. The corpse of Jesus is the "embodiment" of the Son of man. It speaks truth. After Jesus' arrest, the vulnerability associated with human life was symbolized in the young man who, when seized, flees naked—fully exposed (14:52). We may assume that, because the soldiers "divided his garments among them" (15:24), Jesus' corpse is naked also. The difference between Jesus and the young man is that Jesus is dead.

We shall see below that the kingdom of God does not finally take place by means of a ministry to the corpse of Jesus. Mark does seem to suggest, however, that searching for the kingdom of God by asking for the corpse of Jesus is a legitimate starting point: the fallen body of Jesus, Son of man, graphically portrays the consequences of feelings of exclusivism and entitlement to power. The consequences are violence and death. Understanding the human condition, which is generated by taking the corpse of Jesus, is the beginning of participation in the kingdom of God. Taking the corpse of Jesus for burial cultivates an understanding of the conditions in which we find ourselves. Participation in the kingdom of God is brought to fruition when, understanding the human condition, we respond appropriately in an effort to ease human suffering. The appropriate response is not, however, found in the tomb. As the young man will now declare, it is found in Galilee, the fountainhead of Mark's Christology.

The Empty Tomb

Recall again the earlier story of the anointing of Jesus that opened the Passion story: "And truly, I say to you, wherever the gospel is preached in the whole world, what she has done will be told in memory of her" (14:9). The Passion story now concludes with an episode concernng the non-anointing of Jesus' corpse. We naturally conclude that the story of the anointing provides an appropriate backdrop against which the story of the non-anointing, the empty-tomb story, must be contrasted.

A comparison of Mark 14:3–9 with 16:1–8 reveals that at least six components of the empty-tomb story have counterparts in the episode of Jesus' being anointed in the house of the leper by a woman. And yet we should also note that each counterpart is also different. The leper's house corresponds to the tomb. Both are regarded as taboo by design of the Pentateuch; both are unclean (see Leviticus 13 and Num. 19:11). But there is a difference as well: people live in

the slum; it is not empty. The tomb, however, is empty; the dead do
not live there. Second, there is the contrast between the clothing of
the leper and the clothing of the young man. The leper's clothes are
torn (Lev. 13:45); the young man is "dressed in a white robe" (Mark
16:5). Third, there is one woman at the house of the leper, but three
women at the grave. Fourth, the one woman succeeds in anointing
Jesus; the three women fail. Fifth, at the leper's house, there is
indignation over the anointing, as opposed to the trembling and
astonishment associated with the failure to anoint in the tomb.
Finally, in the leper's house, Jesus proclaims that on the occasion of
the preaching of the gospel, the woman's deeds will be "told in
memory of her" (14:9), whereas the three women fail to share the
good news upon departing from the tomb (16:8).

The negative components of the empty-tomb story, then, point to
the positive components in the story of the house of the leper—the
episode that memorializes the gospel (14:9)—"in memory of her."
This may mean that the empty-tomb story serves as the backdrop
against which the anointing episode is contrasted. Narratively the
anointing episode (14:3–9) enables us to interpret the empty-tomb
story (16:1–8).

Previously we noted that the search for the kingdom of God can
begin with asking for the corpse of Jesus (15:43). This initiates
reflection concerning the human condition. Although Jesus' burial
takes place on "the day of Preparation" at evening, that is, after the
Sabbath has actually begun, no further ministry concerning the
corpse of Jesus takes place on the Sabbath itself. Instead, at the conclusion of the Sabbath, the three women bring "spices, so that they
might go and anoint him" (16:1). They approach the tomb "very
early on the first day of the week . . . when the sun had risen" (16:2).
On the journey to the tomb, the three women express concern over
the stone that has been rolled "against the door of the tomb" as security (15:46): "Who will roll away the stone for us from the door of
the tomb?" (16:3). When they arrive at the tomb, however, they
discover that the stone has been "rolled back—it was very large"
(16:4). The women proceed into the tomb. Here they discover not
the corpse of Jesus, which they expect to find; they discover "a

young man sitting on the right side, dressed in a white robe" (16:5).
The women are amazed. Jesus' fallen corpse is absent; the anointing
of his corpse will not take place:

> And he said to them, "Do not be amazed; you seek Jesus of Nazareth,
> who was crucified. He has risen, he is not here; see the place where
> they laid him." (16:6)

The meaning of the failure to anoint the corpse of Jesus begins to
become clear. Whereas the search for the kingdom of God can begin
with asking for the corpse of Jesus, participation in the kingdom of
God does not finally take place through a ministry to the dead. It
takes place through a ministry to the living human being. Mark
makes this point in several ways. For one thing, the anointing has
already taken place: Jesus had said, "She has anointed my body
beforehand for burying" (14:8b). The anointing of Jesus in the
house of the leper symbolizes Jesus' association with the woman and
the leper as well as their association with Jesus. The way Mark suggests that appropriate ministry is not to the dead but to the living is
through the presence of the young man at the tomb. This young
man is fully alive and fully clothed. Furthermore, he is the second
young man we encounter in the Passion story. His presence at the
tomb reminds us of the young man in the garden at the arrest.
Unlike the young man at the tomb, the young man at the arrest is
naked. We are reminded of this young man when we read of the
young man in the tomb, just as we are aware of the leper's torn
clothes. The condition of the young man who is naked is a graphic
reminder of the vulnerability associated with the ministry of Jesus
precisely because it is a ministry to the living human being.

We see this even more clearly in the instructions that the young
man issues:

> But go, tell his disciples and Peter that he is going before you to Gali-
> lee; there you will see him, as he told you. (16:7)

Coupled with Jesus' absence from the tomb is his journey to Galilee.
Galilee is not a tomb; Galilee is a place where people live. The res-
urrection links the fallen corpse of the crucified Christ with Galilee.
And the fallen corpse embodies the situation in which we find

ourselves—the very reason for ministry. But ministry is not to the fallen corpse; the women cannot anoint the dead body of Jesus. Rather the fallen corpse of the crucified Christ ministers. The fallen corpse ministers to the living because it discloses the human condition so graphically. And because it discloses the human condition so graphically, the fallen corpse generates ministry—a ministry of people with people.

By associating the resurrection with Galilee, Mark is narratively making a negative statement with regard to Jerusalem. As Galilee is the seat of unorthodox messianic ideas, Mark seems to suggest that the Christology espoused and practiced in Jerusalem is a failure. We see this in Mark's treatment both of the religious officials of Judaism and of Jesus' disciples. Judas, for example, hands over Jesus to a crowd from the authorities (14:44–45). And Simon Peter, who has harbored grandiose views of Israel's Messiah, has also tried to negotiate a position for himself as an entitled recipient of special favor. The Christology that Jesus practices totally shatters Peter's long-held expectations. As far as Peter is concerned, the Christology that Jesus practices is a failure. Consequently, Peter fails to follow Jesus.

And yet it is to Peter himself that the three women are instructed by the young man to issue a reminder: "He is going before you to Galilee; there you will see him, as he told you" (16:7; cf. 14:28). For Peter, there is hope in that the gospel is designated for him in spite of his failure. The gospel of Jesus Christ has embraced the woman and the leper. The gospel of Jesus Christ has embraced those who seize Jesus in order to kill him. And the gospel embraces Peter, who has forsaken Jesus. The gospel is for the living; it embraces the living.

By suggesting that ministry is to the living, Mark does not diminish the risk to the follower of Jesus one iota. There is no magic. There is no protection. No invincibility is guaranteed. There is nothing to protect us from the grave. Wherever authentic ministry takes place, there is great risk that what happened to Jesus could happen to the believer.

Frightening? Indeed. For this reason, upon hearing the good news, the women are filled with trembling and astonishment, and in fear they flee. Just as the disciples "all forsook him, and fled" (14:50), so also the women, upon hearing the words of the young man, "fled from the tomb" (16:8). And having fled the tomb, they are utterly silent. They completely fail to share the good news, "for they were afraid" (16:8).

PREPARING TO
PREACH AND TEACH

Appropriately, this represents the conclusion of the Gospel of Mark. The conclusion is appropriate because the empty-tomb story leaves the reader with no illusions. Christianity does not involve girding oneself with a sword. And being a Christian does not bring relief from fear. Instead, being a Christian involves participation in the kingdom of God—a kingdom where the believer knowingly raises the cup and celebrates the practice of mutual receptivity, a kingdom where our ability to defend ourselves is not necessarily strong.

The story as we have it concludes with the notion of fear: "And they went out and fled from the tomb, for trembling and astonishment had come upon them; and they said nothing to anyone, for they were afraid" (16:8). For the modern reader, this is a curious way for a story to end. Why? Because the modern reader, familiar with post-resurrection appearance stories in Matthew, Luke, and John, has learned to expect something different from what happens here in Mark. Indeed, this seems to have been a problem for early Christianity, resulting in the addition, by a later editor, of Mark 16:9–20. However, given the original ending of 16:8, Mark is the only Gospel that ends on the note of fear.

In view of this situation, both preacher and teacher are presented with a significant opportunity to explore the fear associated with following Jesus. The sermon or Bible study might properly begin with a question: Why the fear? Why does the story end in this curious way? The three women have been following Jesus. And yet, in the end, they fail to tell the good news. Why? What factors contribute to their fear? And what is the nature of the fear associated with the practice of Christianity?

Answers to these questions are found in those portions of the Passion story that lead to the empty tomb. They have to do with the events that take place in the leper's house and the response to conflict that Jesus initiates in the upper room and practices in the garden. They have to do with Jesus' conduct in the temple and the palace. And they have to do with the cross itself. There is fear associated with following Jesus because following Jesus is a practice that involves great risk. The story of the empty tomb does not signal the supplanting of vulnerability. It does not symbolize the dawn of invincibility. Instead, it reminds us, by way of contrast with the leper's house, of the situation in which we find ourselves today: our community, like Mark's, is fragmented by social ostracism and the fear generated by the specter of betrayal and violence.

The sermon or study that explores the problem of fear might begin with a broad look at the Passion story, bringing to focus the causes of fear. By summarizing those episodes that lead to the empty-tomb story, the sermon or study would treat the empty-tomb story in context as the final chapter in the Passion story. This eliminates the danger of regarding the empty-tomb story as the episode that negates and undercuts all that has brought the reader to the empty-tomb story.

The second movement might re-create the situation of the three women looking on from afar (15:40–41). In this way, the listener is invited to see and participate in what follows.

In keeping with the narrative contour of the story, the third movement would focus on Joseph of Arimathea (15:42–47). This movement is significant because, in approaching Pilate to ask for the corpse of Jesus, Joseph of Arimathea takes courage (15:43). Joseph is looking for the kingdom of God. Participation in the kingdom of God can properly begin, as we have seen, with the reflection on human suffering that asking for the corpse of Jesus initiates. This takes courage. In the context of the Passion story, courage is understood not as the opposite of fear but rather as the partner of fear. To take courage is not to suggest that because one is a Christian one is free from fear. It means that the Christian is called to guard against being possessed or driven by fear. From the story, from Joseph of Arimathea, from the woman who anoints Jesus, and especially from Jesus himself, the Christian is called to take courage to act appropriately against fear.

The episode regarding Joseph of Arimathea prepares the listener to hear the fourth and final movement of the sermon, the story of the empty tomb. The story should be told with the appropriate details that we have noted in the previous section. With Joseph, the listener has been encouraged to see, to know, and to understand the reality of human suffering. The listener understands that involving oneself in an effort to ease and transform suffering confronts the believer with a liability that provokes fear. Nevertheless, understanding fear and encouraged by the story itself, the listener, with the disciples and Peter, is directed to Galilee. There, the corpse of Jesus, which embodies the human condition, reminds us of the reality of human suffering. We too are thus invited to receive, embrace, and include the socially ostracized, so that as the kingdom of God our community might become one body.

Conclusion:
The Passion as Story

The title of this book suggests that the Passion as recorded by Mark is most appropriately understood as story. As story, the Passion has a composer, whom we call Mark.[15] We have shown that as a composer Mark has selected certain materials. The selection is orderly and is executed with great care. It is no accident that in Mark's Passion story we see certain groups, and within the groups, certain people are featured. By narratively contrasting the appropriate groups and characters, the author constructs the story's meaning. We see, for example, the Twelve. Within the Twelve, Mark singles out three, Peter, James, and John, and from the three, one—Peter. Judas is likewise singled out from the Twelve. The council is divided into the chief priests, the scribes, and the elders, with the chief priests taking the lead. From the chief priests we have the high priest. From the council, we have Joseph of Arimathea. Joseph of Arimathea may be contrasted with Judas. One centurion is singled out from the soldiers. Of the bystanders, one draws his sword. Bystanders are contrasted with passers-by, the Twelve with the council, and the council with the crowd.

There are also certain dramatis personae whom Mark singles out and who may be contrasted. There are three Simons—Simon the leper, Simon Peter, and Simon of Cyrene. There are numerous pairs of opposites: the high priest versus Pilate, one woman versus three women, the young man at the arrest versus the young man at the tomb, Peter versus the maid as opposed to Jesus versus the high priest, Simon of Cyrene the father versus Mary the mother, Simon of Cyrene versus Joseph of Arimathea, Jesus versus Barabbas, Jesus versus the two robbers, Jesus versus David, and Jesus versus Elijah.

Specific times and places are also singled out. Indeed, we have divided the story into pericopes coinciding with seven different places. In addition, we see the leper's house versus the tomb, both of which are regarded as taboo. We also see the upper room versus Gethsemane, Golgotha versus temple and palace, the temple versus the courtyard, Jerusalem versus Galilee, and Jerusalem and Galilee versus Cyrene. We likewise see time being marked: two days before the Passover, the first day of the Passover, the day of Preparation, the Sabbath, the first day of the week, cockcrow, and the third, sixth, and ninth hours.

We have also noted that Mark has selected certain passages from the Old Testament that are of value in the composition of the story because they reflect certain patterns of meaning Mark wishes to convey. Having selected the appropriate materials, Mark then weaves them together in a way that is aesthetically effective. The story has beauty. It captures the imagination. It speaks to the situation in which we find ourselves. It enables the listener to hear and understand things he or she has not heard before. It enables one to see and understand the human condition in a way that, until the hearing of the story, was not possible. Furthermore, it enables the human being to see and understand ways in which the human condition can be transformed.

What gives the story its authority is not that the story narrates something that happened. What gives the story its authority is that it conveys the human condition and provides for its transformation. Given this situation, the Passion story deserves to be read, studied, heard, and preached. The Passion story mediates the kingdom of God in the way of the cross. Anyone who participates in the way of the cross expresses his or her willingness to receive a fellow human being; the believer communicates the gospel through action. Consequently, the believer who preaches, teaches, or tells the story with authenticity does not alienate or victimize the listener. Instead, the believer conveys his or her empathic understanding of the situations in which the story finds listener or student. Conveying an understanding of and receptivity to the listener's or student's situation, the believer's telling of the Passion story mediates the kingdom-of-God vision to the hearer. The one who has heard the story then moves into the ordinary world with the feeling of having been understood and an understanding of both the dynamics of conflict and a better approach to its resolution.

To suggest that the Passion is story, as opposed to a mere representation of historical fact, is to suggest that the Passion is the imaginative communication of truth. It is composed, formed, and shaped by an author. And because it is composed, formed, and shaped, it is capable of forming and shaping the community today. The story forms our community. The story shapes our destiny. The story re-creates the situation of conflict. The story uncovers the reasons for conflict. The story exposes and confronts conventional approaches to the resolution of conflict by providing an alternative approach. The story symbolizes the kingdom of God, the kingdom of mutual receptivity. The story facilitates our vision of Christ as one who receives his takers, presenting himself to them as vulnerable, transforming their act of taking into an act of receiving. By re-creating in the imagination of the listener a more appropriate response to conflict, the story gives rise to faith.

The story is the church's gift. It helps the church to respond more appropriately to those who provoke conflict. The gift is shared. The church becomes not only the receiver of the gift, but the giver of the gift as well. The new recipient is the one with whom the Christian, understanding the story, has contact. Embraced by the gift of the story, the Christian is enabled to embrace another. The gift takes root in the hearts of the people of the world. And the people find the grace in their hearts to participate in the kingdom of God.

Notes

1. Joachim Jeremias, *Jerusalem in the Time of Jesus*, trans. F. H. and C. H. Cave (Philadelphia: Fortress Press, 1969), 359, 372–73.

2. Ibid., 374.

3. Ibid., 7.

4. Ibid.

5. Ibid.

6. Ibid., 72.

7. Ibid., 73.

8. Ibid., 61.

9. Ibid., 62.

10. Joachim Jeremias, *The Prayers of Jesus* (Philadelphia: Fortress Press, 1967), 58.

11. One difficulty that faces the interpreter has to do with the question, Is Peter unwilling to follow Jesus or unable? In the Passion story, Peter initially expresses his willingness to stand with Jesus (Mark 14:31). And when Jesus first finds Peter sleeping, Jesus says to Peter that "the spirit is indeed willing, but the flesh is weak" (14:38). To suggest that the flesh is weak does suggest a certain kind of inability. It is not, however, an inability that is associated with misunderstanding. It seems, rather, that because of the threat to their lives, the disciples are finally unwilling to follow Jesus. Were the disciples merely unable (in the sense that they do not understand), they could not be held responsible for their actions.

12. The reader may have noted the subtitle to this chapter: "Intimations of Eden." At this point, an explanation is in order. The stories both of Gethsemane and of Eden are garden stories. As we can now see, both focus on the problem of temptation. In addition, both feature an act of taking. And in the end, the dramatis personae of both stories leave the garden.

13. For another discussion of this problem, see Krister Stendahl, *Holy Week Preaching* (Philadelphia: Fortress Press, 1985), 9–12.

14. Finding significant background information concerning Simon of Cyrene can be difficult. We know from Jeremias, *Jerusalem*, 71, that some

Cyrenians "converted to Christianity." That Cyrene is a far-off country may be Mark's narrative way of suggesting a kind of universalization: the relevance of the gospel for not only Jerusalem and Galilee but also the four corners of the earth.

15. Were this book primarily for scholars, I would have used the word "fiction" in the same sense in which it is used by Robert W. Funk in "The Issue of Jesus," *Forum* 1/1 (1985): 11.